MAJOR ISSUES IN THE LIFE AND WORK OF C. G. JUNG

Edited by

William Schoenl

University Press of America, Inc.
Lanham • New York • London

Copyright © 1996 by
University Press of America,® Inc.
4720 Boston Way
Lanham, Maryland 20706

3 Henrietta Street
London, WC2E 8LU England

Library of Congress Cataloging-in-Publication Data

Major issues in the life and work of C. G. Jung / edited by William
Schoenl.
p.   cm.
Includes bibliographical references.
1. Jung, C. G. (Carl Gustav), 1875-1961. 2. Freud, Sigmund, 1856-
1939--Friends and associates. 3. Psychoanalysts--Austria--Biography.
4. Jungian psychology--History. 5. Psychoanalysis--History. I.
Schoenl, William J.
BF 109.J8M343   1996   150.19'54'092 --dc20   96-32905   CIP

ISBN 0-7618-0469-2 (cloth: alk. ppr.)
ISBN 0-7618-0470-6 (pbk: alk. ppr.)

To Erma and Bill,
my mother and father

Contents

Preface

In patterns of cloud's shadow and sun on a Swiss mountain lake we may see C. G. Jung's reflection–and our own. An alternative to Freud Jung had his detractors and his admirers. If the former were too critical the latter sometimes overlooked flaws. This volume presents major issues in his life and work. Why did he break with Freud? Was he empirical–or mystical? Was he anti-Nazi or, for a time, "a Nazi sympathizer"? Why was his *Answer to Job* controversial? Though the list is not exhaustive each issue remains significant.

This work was written with the conviction that the time has come to frame the issues through writings by Jung and distinguished authors on Jung and to give both sides and new Jungian perspectives that consider both sides. It provides an objective, historical approach and it is based in part on seminars in history that I have offered at Michigan State University. I am indebted to participants for insights and suggestions. We hope that this book may stimulate further inquiry and readers may come to their own conclusions on the issues.

I. Why did Jung break with Freud? Though Jung and Freud broke in 1913 the rift was already opening between them during the previous year: They had disagreed over Freud's strictly sexual interpretation of libido and his view of incest. Jung regarded Freud as authoritarian and dogmatic, while Freud felt that Jung was attempting to overturn him as a father figure. In a letter to Freud, December 3, 1912–our first selection–Jung put their differences openly and strongly. Two letters between Ernest Jones and Freud written shortly after Jung's letter of December 3 comprise the second selection. They provide a Freudian view of Jung's differences with the founder of psychoanalysis. The complete correspondence of Freud and Jones was only recently published (1993). Jung personally commented on his break with Freud to his students in his Seminar in Analytical Psychology, 1925. In Zurich it became the standard Jungian view of the break. The Notes of the Seminar were not published until 1989. The fourth selection is a current perspective from a recent article in *The Journal of Analytical Psychology*–a major Jungian journal. While not denying Jung's view that Freud was authoritarian and dogmatic, Brian Feldman sees Jung's infancy and childhood as a significant influence.

II. Was Jung empirical–or mystical? Jung was often charged with being non-empirical and mystical, and, as often, he asserted that he was empirical. Our first selection is from his Terry Lectures in religion and science at Yale University in 1937–published as *Psychology and Religion* (1938)–in which he held that his approach was empirical. Freudians and behaviorists criticized Jung's psychology as non-empirical. His psychology went largely unaccepted in the academic world. Walter Kaufmann, well-known for his works on Nietzsche, provides a severe pro-Freudian criticism of Jung in the next selection taken from his *Discovering the Mind*, Volume 3: *Freud versus Adler and Jung* (1980). J. J. Clarke's *In Search of Jung* (1992) provides a contemporary perspective on the charges against Jung. Clark enumerates the attacks against Jung's work over the years and illustrates a defense. Richard Noll's *The Jung Cult: Origins of a Charismatic Movement* (1994) is a recent challenge to the view that Jung was empirical–and to the theory of the collective unconscious. In a review in *Psychological Perspectives* (Spring-Summer 1995), Barbara Stephens assesses its strengths and weaknesses.

III. Was Jung anti-Nazi or, for a time, "a Nazi sympathizer"? Jung has had detractors who were as certain of the latter as admirers were equally sure of the former. Who is right? Is the matter much more complex? Our first selection is from Jung's somewhat ambiguously worded editorial in the journal of the General Medical Society for Psychotherapy in December 1933–the year the Nazis came to power in Germany. Subsequently, charges arose that Jung was a Nazi sympathizer and anti-Semitic. Our next selection is from Geoffrey Cocks' *Psychotherapy in the Third Reich* (2nd edition, forthcoming) in which the author investigates the matter of Jung and psychotherapy in Germany from 1933 to 1940. Recently some new material concerning Jung, anti-Semitism, and the Nazis has been discovered. Our third selection is from Jung's letter to Mary Mellon, September 24, 1945, in which Jung denied that he was ever a Nazi, but his letter left the charge of anti-Semitism open. The matter of anti-Semitism has cast shadows over relations between Jungians and Freudians virtually since the break with Freud and, especially, since the time of Nazi Germany. In their *Lingering Shadows: Jungians, Freudians, and Anti-Semitism* (1991) Aryeh Maidenbaum and Stephen Martin brought together many of the views that have been expressed on the matter. Our fourth selection is from Maidenbaum's Preface to this work. More than anyone else Andrew Samuels has continued the investigation into the questions: Was Jung anti-Semitic and, for a time, "a Nazi sympathizer"? The fifth selection from his recent book, *The Political Psyche* (1993), includes some new materials and it is work that cannot be ignored.

IV. Why was Jung's *Answer to Job* controversial? In the last decade of his life no work by Jung was so controversial as his *Answer to Job* (German ed. 1952; English ed. 1954). Our first selection is from his letter of November 8, 1954, to his friend J. B. Priestley–the English novelist and playwright who had promoted a greater awareness of Jung's psychology in Britain. In it Jung tells Priestley why he felt the work was controversial. Victor White, a Dominican friar and theologian, became a close friend of Jung. A disagreement arose between them, however, over White's view of evil as privation of good and they fell out with each other. In March 1955 in *Blackfriars* White published sharp criticisms of Jung's *Answer to Job*: Our second selection is from it. H. L. Philp corresponded with Jung on the problem of evil. He eventually became convinced there were some serious weaknesses in *Answer to Job*. The third selection is from his *Jung and the Problem of Evil* (1958). Kathleen Newton gives a current perspective incorporating the most recent scholarship in her article in *The Journal of Analytical Psychology* (October 1993). She assesses the personal and the archetypal dimensions in *Answer to Job*.

As green water shades to blue, shallows into deep, so, too, Jung's life and work remain.

William Schoenl
Spring 1996

I. Why Did Jung Break with Freud?

1. Jung's View

Jung to Freud, December 3, 1912:*

*Freud and Jung broke in 1913 but the rift was already opening
between them during the previous year. Jung had disagreed with
Freud's strictly sexual interpretation of libido; he was conceiving
it to be psychic energy. He had also disagreed with Freud's view
of incest: Freud had taken incest literally, while Jung saw it
symbolically. Moreover, personal differences were emerging. Jung
had come to regard Freud as authoritarian and dogmatic; Freud
felt that Jung was attempting to overturn him as a father figure.
The following letter from Jung to Freud on December 3, 1912,
put their differences openly and strongly.*

My very best thanks for one passage in your letter [of November
29], where you speak of a "bit of neurosis" you haven't got rid of.
This "bit" should, in my opinion, be taken very seriously indeed
because, as experience shows, it leads "usque ad instar voluntariae

*From *The Freud/Jung Letters: The Correspondence between Sigmund Freud
and C. G. Jung*, ed. William McGuire, tr. Ralph Manheim and R. F. C.
Hull, Bollingen Series XCIV, pp. 525-527. Copyright ©1974 by Princeton
University Press and Routledge (London). Reprinted by permission of
Princeton University Press and Routledge.

mortis" [to the semblance of a voluntary death]. I have suffered from this bit in my dealings with you, though you haven't seen it and didn't understand me properly when I tried to make my position clear. If these blinkers were removed you would, I am sure, see my work in a very different light. As evidence that you–if I may be permitted so disrespectful an expression–*underestimate* my work by a very wide margin, I would cite your remark that "without intending it, I have solved the riddle of all mysticism, showing it to be based on the symbolic utilization of complexes that have outlived their function."

My dear Professor, forgive me again, but this sentence shows me that you deprive yourself of the possibility of understanding my work by your underestimation of it. You speak of this insight as though it were some kind of pinnacle, whereas actually it is at the very bottom of the mountain. This insight has been self-evident to us for years. Again, please excuse my frankness. It is only occasionally that I am afflicted with the purely human desire to be understood *intellectually* and not be measured by the yardstick of neurosis.

As for this bit of neurosis, may I draw your attention to the fact that you open *The Interpretation of Dreams* with the mournful admission of your own neurosis–the dream of Irma's injection–identification with the neurotic in need of treatment. Very significant.

Our analysis [during our trip to America in 1909], you may remember, came to a stop with your remark that you "could not submit to analysis *without losing your authority*." These words are engraved on my memory as a symbol of everything to come. I haven't eaten *my* words, however.

I am writing to you now as I would write *to a friend*–this is *our* style. I therefore hope you will not be offended by my Helvetic bluntness. One thing I beg of you: take these statements as an *effort to be honest* and do not apply the depreciatory Viennese criterion of egoistic striving for power or heaven knows what other insinuations from the world of the father complex. This is just what I have been hearing on all sides these days, with the result that I am forced to the painful conclusion that the majority of psychoanalysts misuse psychoanalysis for the purpose of devaluing others and their progress by insinuations about complexes (as though that explained anything. A wretched theory!). A particularly preposterous bit of nonsense now going the rounds is that my libido theory [which rejected a strictly sexual interpretation of libido and regarded it as psychic energy] is the product of anal erotism. When I consider *who* cooked up this "theory" I fear for the future of analysis.

I want no infantile outpourings of libidinal appreciation or admiration from psychoanalysts, merely an understanding of my ideas. The pity of it is that psychoanalysts are just as supinely dependent on psychoanalysis as our opponents are on their belief in authority. Anything that might make them think is written off as a complex. This protective function of psychoanalysis badly needed unmasking.

2. Freudian View

Ernest Jones to Freud, December 5, 1912:*

The following letters between Ernest Jones and Freud were written shortly after Jung's letter of December 3. They provide a Freudian view of Jung's differences with Freud. Jones was a close associate of Freud in the English-speaking world–and, later, became his biographer. They regarded Jung's behavior as neurotic rebellion. An interesting point in the letters is that Freud admits to some homosexual feeling for Jung. The complete correspondence of Freud and Jones was only recently published (1993).

I enclose a curious letter from Jung which has been sent on from Wales; it was written before Munich. He gives now a new excuse for his behaviour, namely that he has had to neglect his duty towards himself (and therefore does towards his friends). There are some words I cannot read. Would you ask my wife, who has an aptitude for deciphering handwriting, to write them in, and to return the letter to me. (That is better than wasting your time). I have also had an excellently long account from Brill, which gave me many suggestions. The whole thing is fitting together like a Chinese puzzle, and it would not be hard to make a pretty full psychoanalysis of Jung's attitude. Did Brill tell you that he maintains *you* have a severe neurosis?

*From *The Complete Correspondence of Sigmund Freud and Ernest Jones, 1908-1939*, ed. R. Andrew Paskauskas (Cambridge, Mass. and London, Eng.: Belknap Press of Harvard University Press, 1993), pp. 180, 182. Reprinted by permission of Harvard University Press and Mark Paterson & Associates (England).

Another beautiful projection. Jung lays great stress on making psychoanalysis more pleasant and acceptable, therefore more "workable" (Shades of William James; what an honest man to have his name invoked for the support of such an idea!). He will save psychoanalysis in your despite (do you know this idiom?). A word of August Hoch's gives the key to the whole situation. He speaks of Jung's views as being a "deliverance". Jung is going to save the world, another Christ (with certainly Anti-semitism combined). The world is trembling with fear because the *böse Vater* [evil father] has found out their secret thoughts, their incest wishes and infantile sexuality. But the gallant St. George steps forward and reassures the world. "Continue with your infantile sexuality, which is not sexual, and your incest wishes, which are not incestuous. Such things are quite innocent and harmless, and now that I have saved you you need no longer fear." Now I understand better the remark he made to me three years ago in Zurich, that you would destroy your own work by going to extremes but that he would save it (or words to that effect).

From which I would make the prognosis: that he will be willing to suffer at the father's hands, like Christ, and will be *scheinbar un-terw[ü]rfig* [seemingly subservient]; that as psychoanalysis is now his, being saved by him, he will not desert it or break with the movement.

What do you think of all this phantasy?

Freud to Jones, December 8, 1912:
I thank you for your very just remarks about Jung. . . . In fact he behaves like a perfect fool, he seems to be Christ himself, and in the particular things he says there is always something of the *"Lausbub"* [rascal]. But he acted nicely at Munich, got a severe chastisement there, and as he considers psychoanalysis as his own and his position against me is far from indifference I expect as you do that he will stay with us. The letters I get from him are remarkable, changing from tenderness to overbearing insolence. He wants treatment, unfortunately by my last attack I have lost [a] portion of my authority. There must be some psychic element in this attack which besides was largely fundamented on fatigue, bad sleep and smoking, for I cannot forget that 6 and 4 years ago I have suffered from very similar though not so intense symptoms in the *same* room of the Parkhotel; in every case I had to leave the table. I saw Munich first when I visited Fliess during his illness (you remember: "Propyläeen" in the *Traumdeutung*) and this town seems to have acquired a strong connection with my

relation to this man. There is some piece of unruly homosexual feeling at the root of the matter. When Jung in his last letter again hinted at my "neurosis" I could find no better expeditive than proposing that every analyst should attend to his own neurosis more than to the others's. After all I think we have to be kind and patient with Jung and as old Oliver said, keep our powder dry. I restricted myself to the remark against Jung, that I do not think *he* has been a sufferer by my neurosis. In any case, there is a suspicious amount of dishonesty, want of simplicity and frankness I mean in his constitution (Stekel would continue thus:...).

3. Notes of the Seminar in 1925

C. G. Jung*

Jung commented on his break with Freud to his students in his Seminar in Analytical Psychology, 1925. In Zurich it became the standard Jungian view of the break. Cary F. de Angulo, later Baynes, compiled the Notes of the Seminar. Reviewed and corrected by Jung they were privately issued, but not published. Jung published less personal comments in German in 1929; the latter appeared in English as "Freud and Jung: Contrasts" in his popular Modern Man in Search of a Soul *(1933). The Notes of the Seminar in 1925 were not published until 1989.*

Through this book on dementia praecox I came to Freud. We met in 1906. The first day I met him it was at one o'clock in the afternoon, and we talked steadily for thirteen hours. He was the first man of real importance I had seen; no one else could compare with him. I found him extremely shrewd, intelligent, and altogether remarkable. But my first impressions of him were somewhat confused; I could not quite make him out. I found him, though, absolutely serious about his sex theory, and in his attitude there was nothing trivial to be found. It made a great impression on me, but still I had grave doubts. I told him this, and whenever I did, he always said it was because I had not had enough experience. It was a fact that in those days I had not had enough experience upon which to

*From Jung, C. G., *Analytical Psychology: Notes of the Seminar Given in 1925*, ed. William McGuire, Bollingen Series XCIX, pp. 19-25. Copyright ©1989 by Princeton University Press and Routledge (London). Reprinted by permission of Princeton University Press and Routledge.

form a critique. I could see that this sexual theory was enormously important to Freud, both personally and philosophically, but I could not make out whether it came from a personal bias or not, so I went away with a doubt in my mind about the whole situation.

Another impression I got in connection with this seriousness of Freud with respect to his theory of sexuality was this: He invariably sneered at spirituality as being nothing but repressed sexuality, and so I said if one were committed fully to the logic of that position, then one must say that our whole civilization is farcical, nothing but a morbid creation due to repressed sexuality. He said, "Yes, so it is, and its being so is just a curse of fate we cannot help." My mind was quite unwilling to settle there, but still I could not argue it out with him.

A third impression of those days involves things that became clear to me only much later, things that I thought out fully only after our friendship was gone. When Freud talked of sexuality it was as though he were talking of God–as a man would talk who had undergone a conversion. It was like the Indians talking of the sun with tears in their eyes. I remember one Indian coming up softly behind me while I was looking at the mountain over the pueblo, and saying quite suddenly in my ear, "Don't you think all life is coming from the mountain?" It was just in that way that Freud talked of sexuality. A peculiar emotional quality would come into his face, and the cause of it I was at a loss to understand. Finally I seemed to make it out through the consideration of something else that remained obscure to me then, namely Freud's bitterness. One might say Freud consists of bitterness, every word being loaded with it. His attitude was the bitterness of the person who is entirely misunderstood, and his manner always seemed to say, "If they don't understand they must be stamped into Hell." I noticed this in him the first time I met him, and always saw it in him, but I could not find the connection with his attitude toward sexuality.

The explanation seems to me to be this: Freud, for all his repudiation of spirituality, has in reality a mystical attitude toward sexuality. When one protested to him that a certain poem could not be understood on a sexual basis exclusively, he would say, "No, certainly not, that is psychosexuality." But when analyzing the poem, he would pull out this thread and that, and so on until nothing was left but sexuality. Now I think sexuality is a double concept to him, on the one side the mystical element, on the other mere sexuality, but the latter is the only thing that comes out in his terminology because he will not admit he has the other side. That he has the other side, I think, is obvious from the way he showed his emotions. And so he is forever defeating his own purpose. He wants to teach that sexuality contains spirituality looked at from within, but he uses only concretistic sex terminology and conveys just the wrong idea. His bitterness comes from this fact of constantly working against himself, for there is no bitterness worse than that of a man who is his own worst enemy.

Freud is blind to the dualism of the unconscious. He does not know that the thing that wells up has an inside and an outside, and that if you talk only of the latter you speak of the shell alone. But there is nothing to be done about this conflict in him; the only chance would be if he could have an experience that would make him see spirituality working inside the shell. However, his intellect would then inevitably strip it to "mere" sexuality. I tried to present to him cases showing other factors than sexual ones but always he would have it that there was nothing there save repressed sexuality.

As I said, such terribly bitter people are always those who work against themselves. When I work against myself I project the uncertainty and terror that I feel. If I am to avoid this, the one thing to settle is myself. Freud does not know that the unconscious produces a factor to counteract the monistic principle to which he has given himself over. I find him a tragic figure, for he is a great man, but it is a fact that he runs away from himself. He never asks himself why he has to talk about sex all the time, and in this running away from himself he is like any other artist. In fact, creative people are usually like that.

These thoughts came to me, as I said, chiefly after I had broken with Freud. I give them to you because as you know, my relation to Freud has long since become a matter of public discussion, and so I must present my view of it.

I came away from my first visit to Freud feeling that the sexual factor must be taken most seriously. Somewhat bewildered, I began to look at my cases again and kept pretty quiet. In 1909 Freud and I were both invited to Clark University, and we were together daily for about seven weeks. We analyzed dreams each day, and it was then that I got an impression, a fatal one, of his limitations. I had two dreams out of which he could not make head or tail. Of course I did not mind that, for the very greatest person is going to have that experience with dreams some time or other. It was just a human limitation, and I would never have taken it as a reason for not going on; on the contrary, I wanted very much to go on–I felt myself to be his son. Then something happened which put a stop to it.

Freud had a dream on an important theme which I cannot mention. I analyzed it and said there was more to be said if he would give me some points about his private life. He looked at me with a peculiar expression of suspicion in his eyes and said, "I could tell you more but I can't risk my authority." Then I knew further analysis was impossible because he put authority above truth. I said I would have to stop there, and I never asked him again for material. You must understand that I speak here quite objectively, but I must include this experience with Freud, because it is the most important factor in my relation to him. He could not bear any criticism whatsoever.

As Freud could only partially handle my dreams, the amount of symbolical material in them increased as it always does until it is understood. If one remains with a narrow point of view about the dream material, there comes a feeling of dissociation and one feels blind and deaf. When this happens to an isolated man he petrifies.

On my way back from America, I had a dream that was the origin of my book on the *Psychology of the Unconscious*. In those times I had no idea of the collective unconscious; I thought of the conscious as of a room above, with the unconscious as a cellar underneath and then the earth wellspring, that is, the body, sending up the instincts. These instincts tend to disagree with our conscious ideals and so we keep them down. That is the figure I had always used for myself, and then came this dream which I hope I can tell without being too personal.

I dreamed I was in a medieval house, a big, complicated house with many rooms, passages, and stairways. I came in from the street and went down into a vaulted Gothic room, and from there into a cellar. I thought to myself that now I was at the bottom, but then I found a square hole. With a lantern in my hand I peeped down this hole, and saw stairs leading further down, and down these I climbed. They were dusty stairs, very much worn, and the air was sticky, the whole atmosphere very uncanny. I came to another cellar, this one of very ancient structure, perhaps Roman, and again there was a hole through which I could look down into a tomb filled with prehistoric pottery, bones, and skulls; as the dust was undisturbed, I thought I had made a great discovery. There I woke up.

Freud said this dream meant that there were certain people associated with me whom I wanted dead, and buried under two cellars, but I thought the meaning was entirely elsewhere though I could not make it out. I kept thinking this way: The cellar is the unconscious, but what is the medieval house? This I did not make out until much later. But there was something below both cellars even–that is, remains of prehistoric man. What does that mean? I had a strongly impersonal feeling about the dream. Involuntarily I began to make fantasies about it, though I did not then know anything about the principle of fantasizing in order to bring up unconscious material. I said to myself, "Isn't it fine to make excavations. Where am I going to have a chance to do that?" And actually when I came home I looked up a place where excavations were being made, and went to it.

But of course that did not satisfy me. My thoughts then beginning to turn to the East, I began to read about excavations being made in Babylonia. My interest went to books, and I came upon a German book called *Mythology and Symbolism*. I went through the three or four volumes at top speed, reading like mad, in fact, until I became as bewildered as ever I had been in the clinic. I had left the hospital, by the way, in 1909, after being there eight years, but now it seemed to me I was living in an insane asylum of my own making. I went about with all these fantastic figures: centaurs, nymphs, satyrs, gods and goddesses, as though they were patients and I was analyzing them. I read a Greek or a Negro myth as if a lunatic were telling me his anamnesis–I lost myself in puzzling what it could possibly mean.

Slowly out of all this came the *Psychology of the Unconscious*, for in the midst of it I came upon the Miller fantasies, and they acted like a catalyser upon all the material I had gathered together in my mind. I saw in Miss Miller a person who, like myself, had had mythological fantasies, fantasies and dreams of a thoroughly impersonal character. Their impersonality I readily recognized, as well as the fact that they must come from the lower "cellars," though I did not give the name of collective unconscious to them. This then is the way the book grew up.

While working on the book I was haunted by bad dreams. I feel that I must speak of my dreams even though one is unavoidably personal to a degree when one does so. But dreams have influenced all the important changes in my life and theories. Thus for example I came to study medicine by reason of a dream, it having been my firm intention at first to become an archaeologist. With this in view I had entered my name in the list of students of philosophy at the University, but then came this dream, and I changed everything. At that time, I mean when I was working on the *Psychology of the Unconscious*, all my dreams pointed to a break with Freud. I thought, of course, that he would accept the cellars below his cellar, but the dreams were preparing me for the contrary. Freud could see nothing in the book but resistance to the father, and the point in it to which he took the greatest exception was my contention that the libido is split and produces the thing that checks itself. This to him as a monist was utter blasphemy. From this attitude of Freud's I felt more than ever convinced that his idea of God was placed in sexuality, and that libido is to him only an urge in one direction. As a matter of fact, however, I think it can be shown that there is a will to die as well as a will to live. We prepare ourselves for death when we reach the summit of life; or, to put it in another way, after the age of thirty-five, let us say, we begin to know that cooler winds are blowing–at first we don't understand, but later we cannot escape the meaning.

After this break I had with Freud, the pupils that I had all over the world left me and turned to Freud. They were told that my book was rubbish, and that I was a mystic, and with that the matter was settled. Suddenly I found myself completely isolated. This, however disadvantageous it may have been, had also an advantage for me as an introvert; that is it encouraged the vertical movement of the libido. Cut off from the horizontal movement which activity in the outside world brings, I was driven to investigate fully the things within myself.

When I finished the *Psychology of the Unconscious*, I had a peculiarly lucid moment in which I surveyed my path as far as I had come. I thought: "Now you have the key to mythology and you have the power to unlock all doors." But then something within me said: "Why unlock all these doors?" And then I found myself asking what I had done after all. I had written a book about the hero, I had explained the myths of past peoples, but what about my own myth? I had to admit I had none; I knew theirs but none of my own, nor did anyone else have one today. Moreover, we were without an understanding of the unconscious. Around these reflections, as around a central core, grew all the ideas that came to partial expression in the book on types.

4. Influence of Jung's Infancy and Childhood on the Development of Analytical Psychology

Brian Feldman*

Brian Feldman's recent article in The Journal of Analytical Psychology, *a Jungian journal, provides a current perspective on Jung's break with Freud. While not denying Jung's view that Freud was authoritarian and dogmatic Feldman sees Jung's infancy and childhood as an important influence. It is now possible to see merits in both Freud's and Jung's accounts of the break. Further, some Jungian psychologists have in recent years attached more importance to infancy and childhood than Jung did. So, too, some Freudian psychoanalysts have been revising Freud.*

At the age of 83 Jung made the following observation:

> I have never fully unwound the tangle of my earliest memories. They are like individual shoots of a single underground rhizome, like stations on a road of unconscious development. (Jung 1961, p. 27)

Little has been written concerning Jung's childhood and infancy and its relationship to the development of his thought, although some work was done by a close associate of Jung's, Marie-Louise von

*From Brian Feldman, "Jung's Infancy and Childhood and Its Influence upon the Development of Analytical Psychology," *The Journal of Analytical Psychology*, Vol. 37 (July 1992), pp. 255, 257-258, 261-262, 265-267, 271-273. Reprinted by permission of the publisher: Routledge.

Franz. Von Franz adopts an archetypal approach to Jung's childhood and tends to avoid a personal exploration of Jung's early life. She relates that 'from early childhood his own dreams had contained the most impressive mythological images which could not possibly have been explained through his own personal memories and for which he found explanatory parallels in religious history only many years later' (von Franz 1975, p. 124). Von Franz defines Jung's mythologem as the creative and sees his childhood dreams, fantasies, and ritual behaviours as expressions of archetypal patterns which prefigured his later realization of the Self. When the origins of the Jungian approach are investigated, invariably Jung's relationship with Freud, their meeting, their collaboration, and their eventual painful break become the point of focus. . . .

. . . Jung states in his autobiography that he did not discuss his early childhood with anyone until he was 65 years old. He held on to these memories because they provided him with a secret truth and enabled him to preserve a sense of the privacy and integrity of his developing self. In another vein, the early experiences were so painful and often so emotionally overwhelming and confusing that he felt unsure whether another individual would be able to understand and acknowledge them. The question remains, however, how much this also reflected a tendency on Jung's part to isolate himself from painful affective states. . . .

The first memory which Jung reports is from the age of 2 years. In the analytic literature one's first memory is often accorded a large degree of psychological importance. Freud (1917) comments on Goethe's first childhood memory, and talks about the meaning of the first memory in psychoanalysis. Freud states that 'in every psychoanalytic investigation of a life history, it usually happens that the very recollection to which the patient gives precedence, with which he introduces the story of his life proves to be the most important, the very one that holds the key to the secret pages of his mind' (Freud 1917, p. 149). . . .

With Freud's observations on the importance of first memories in mind, Jung describes his first memory as follows:

> I am lying in a pram, in the shadow of a tree. It is a fine, warm summer day, the sky blue, and golden sunlight darting through green leaves. The hood of the pram has been left up. I have just awakened to the glorious beauty of the day, and have a

sense of indescribable well-being. I see the sun glittering
through the leaves and blossoms of the bushes. Everything is
wholly wonderful, colourful, and splendid. (Jung 1961, p. 21)

This is an ecstatic experience of the sensory world and the world of
nature. What is conspicuously lacking is any mention of the
interpersonal world. Often when conducting analysis with both
adolescents and adults the first memory that is reported involves the
relationship with caregivers, parents, or significant others. Jung's early
memories are largely devoid of people and for the most part are
descriptions of the sensory world and the realm of nature. I was
perplexed by the conspicuous absence of real people in Jung's
descriptions of his infancy. What did this indicate about his early
experience? . . .

While Jung's early experiences had mainly an ecstatic emotional
quality, this emotional tone may have been a defence against
particularly painful affect. The source of this pain was apparently the
significant problems within the Jung family. When Jung was 3 years
old his mother was hospitalized for what appears to have been a
severe depression. She was away from him for several months, and
Jung says that her hospitalization was related to difficulties that were
surfacing in the parental relationship. During his mother's absence he
was taken care of by a maid. He also developed a severe skin rash
which he connected with the separation of his parents and his
mother's hospitalization. . . .

It appears that Jung was unable to identify with his mother's
containing and soothing function. Jung's mother, Emilie Prieswerk,
was a homely woman, described by Jung as having two distinct
personalities, one innocuous and human, the other uncanny. When
the uncanny part emerged it was often unexpected and frightening.
Jung says, 'She would then speak as if talking to herself, but what she
said was aimed at me and usually struck to the core of my being, so
that I was stunned into silence' (Jung 1961, p. 66). At times his
mother seemed dissociated, and Jung was deeply affected by these
experiences. Because of this he did not develop the kind of bond with
his mother that would have led him to evolve the memory of being
securely attached to a mothering figure. He had to turn to the
sensory world for support, as he could hold on to the sensory world
and nature in a more secure manner. He speaks of this period as
follows: 'I was deeply troubled by my mother's being away. From

then on I always felt mistrustful when the word "love" was spoken. The feeling I associated with "woman" was for a long time that of innate unreliability' (Jung 1961, p. 23). . . .

. . . Nevertheless, the dream of the underground phallus is a critically important one for Jung's development [Jung 1961, pp. 26-27]. It is a symbolic rendering of the birth of his creative genius and is I think the experiential foundation of analytical psychology. The dream is also a statement of Jung's 'oedipal phase' of child development. . . .

Jung did not share this dream with anyone until he was 65 years old, and it remained for him one of the most important internal experiences of his life. The dream's intense vividness and sensory quality, as well as the emotional terror it evokes, are impressive. Jung amplified and associated later in life to the dream and felt that it was a representation of a descent into the earth and an archetypal initiation into the secrets of life. Jung saw it as an initiation into 'the secrets of the earth' and 'the realm of darkness'. Jung reports that his intellectual life had an unconscious beginning at that time.

From a developmental perspective this dream also conveys three separate but related issues: (1) Jung's dread of the penis, (2) Jung's fascination with his own phallic excitement, and (3) Jung's terror of encountering the penis inside the mother's body. . . . But if the son goes there, the father's penis that is already there might castrate him, and we know from Jung's own later psychology that the mother's animus can be a castrating phallic force as well. When his mother says in the dream 'beware of the man-eater', she is voicing Jung's concern about potential castration by his combined 'bad' and dangerous internal parents. The dream conveys some of Jung's anxiety about what is going on inside mother's body. His fear of potential castration by the father's penis inside the mother could have made it difficult for him to relate in a productive way to his own childhood sexuality, and this may provide an explanation for his early renunciation of Freud's theory of childhood sexuality. Jung attempted to refute Freud's theory of childhood sexuality by stating that the nutritive function had a greater importance in children than did sexuality. In clinical work with children I have found that bodily experiences which include sexual sensations and fantasies, are very important, and need to be integrated into the analytic treatment if deeper progress is to be made. In his writings Jung tended to minimize the importance of sexuality in early childhood, and this is a deficit in his theory which has needed to be corrected.

From the archetypal standpoint the phallus in the dream is an enormously creative symbol. For the ancient Romans (von Franz 1975) the phallus symbolizes a man's sacred genius, the source of his physical and mental creative powers. The phallus symbolically is the dispenser of all his inspired or brilliant ideas and of his buoyant joy of life. . . .

. . . we can surmise that the parents had a dysfunctional sexual relationship and that his mother was imbued with fear and dread which his father could only partially contain. External evidence of the parents' sexual difficulties was that only one other child was born, a sister, nine years after Jung's birth. This was unusual in Swiss families at that time, especially since both Jung's father and mother came from families with eight children. The development of childhood sexuality is connected with the idea the child has of the parents' sexuality, and children are more secure when they feel their parents are united in a loving sexual way. Jung's concept of sexuality was certainly influenced by this external situation. In Jung's dream his mother calls the phallus the 'man-eater' (potentially the castrator). This might be interpreted by us as well as the child Jung to mean that the father's penis was experienced as dangerous to the mother. Since the parents' relationship was so difficult, evidently estranged, the child Jung must have had an arduous task in developing and integrating his own sense of sexual identity. . . .

. . . The waking fantasy [of God defecating on Basel Cathedral] occurred. . . when he was 12, and began when he was standing in the cathedral square in Basel. Yet this too was a creative solution. I think that this experience also provided the original foundation for Jung's later practice of active imagination as a way of integrating potentially threatening conflicts. Active imagination is a therapeutic technique that Jung evolved whereby a symbolic image is concentrated upon so that fantasy images and affects can be elaborated and reflected upon. It is a type of waking dream taking place in a state of reverie.

Jung describes his 12-year-old experience of fantasy before the Basel cathedral as follows:

One fine summer day . . . I came out of school at noon and went to the cathedral square. The sky was gloriously blue, the day one of radiant sunshine. The roof of the cathedral glittered, the sun sparkling from the new, brightly glazed tiles. I was overwhelmed by the beauty of the sight, and thought: 'The world is beautiful and the church is beautiful, and God made all this and sits above it far away in the blue sky on a golden throne and'

–at this point Jung was unable to go on with his thoughts. For several days he was unable to think what he thought would be a terrible idea. He attempted to try to hold himself together by not thinking the thought. He says:

again and again the forbidden thought, which I did not yet know, tried to break out, and I struggled desperately to fend it off. . . .

I gathered all my courage, as though I were about to leap forthwith into hellfire, and let the thought come. I saw before me the cathedral, the blue sky. God sits on His golden throne, high above the world–and from under the throne an enormous turd falls upon the sparkling new roof, shatters it and breaks the walls of the cathedral asunder.

. . . I felt an enormous, an indescribable relief. Instead of the expected damnation, grace had come upon me, and with it an unutterable bliss such as I had never known. I wept for happiness and gratitude. . . . It was as though I had experienced an illumination. . . . That was what my father had not understood. I thought; he had failed to experience the will of God, had opposed it for the best reasons and out of the deepest faith. And that was why he had never experienced the miracle of grace which heals all and makes all comprehensible. (Jung 1961, pp. 52-57)

I believe Jung's narcissistic rage towards both of his emotionally unresponsive parents was expressed in this fantasy. Jung's father, a clergyman filled with self-doubt about his calling, did not provide Jung with an adequate model for spiritual identification. Jung felt that his father had never known the inner, living experience of God, therefore his faith and belief were empty. Jung says he always had to 'experience and know'. He could not just 'believe', which is what his father wanted him to do although he felt his father really doubted. In the fantasy of God defecating on Basel cathedral Jung symbolically experienced the destruction of the father's world, and for Jung the patriarchal culture as well. Equally, his mother, represented in the fantasy as mother church, was often emotionally unavailable, difficult to reach, and detached. Jung's anger, at the threshold of puberty, was enormous and largely unresolved. Both parents had seriously betrayed him, and he had to turn within himself for support. Although his solutions had a precocious quality, they left him vulnerable throughout his life to deep psychological distress.

There is one more experience, which belongs to Jung's adolescence, which provides the emotional background for his inability to use the mentoring solution as a way out of his disappointment with his parents. At the age of 18 (Beebe, personal communication) Jung was somehow seduced by an older friend of his father's. Jung was later to write to Freud that he felt deeply for Freud but was conflicted by these feelings because he says 'as a boy I was the victim of a sexual assault by a man I once worshipped' (Freud/Jung 1974, p. 95). In later life, when Jung felt let down, abandoned or betrayed, he would fall into dark states of mind, and experienced states of fragmentation and disorganization. His experience with Freud is a case in point. Towards Freud he initially felt a 'veneration' which for Jung took the form of a 'religious crush' (Jung's words). When his relationship with Freud collapsed, he tumbled deeply into the realm of the unconscious, and was able, again through his enormous will and creativity, to give shape to his disintegrated psychic states. This was the period during which his critically important self-analysis took place. Again, it was clear that Jung would always turn, in his hardest times, to himself.

CONCLUSION

Creating his psychological theories was a reparative process for Jung. He could not develop a coherent theory of child development because his own childhood had been so terribly painful, and he did not have the possibility of working through his infantile traumas in a contained analysis as we would think of it today. Rather, Jung delved within himself to find his own healing potential. What he has left us is a remarkable legacy of a creative encounter with the depths of the human spirit. His work has shown how the inner world can compensate for a painful and tormented outer experience in a creative and transformative way.

II: Was Jung Empirical—or Mystical?

1. Psychology and Religion

C. G. Jung*

*Jung was often charged with being non-empirical and mystical or
metaphysical. As often, he asserted that he was empirical. He
was invited to give the Terry Lectures on "Religion in the Light
of Science and Philosophy" at Yale University in 1937, and did
so. They were published under the title* Psychology and Religion
*in 1938. At the outset of his lectures Jung asserts that his
approach is empirical. In the following selection he goes on to
speak of the matter.*

Although I have often been called a philosopher, I am an empiricist and adhere as such to the phenomenological standpoint. I trust
that it does not conflict with the principles of scientific empiricism if
one occasionally makes certain reflections which go beyond a mere
accumulation and classification of experience. As a matter of fact I
believe that experience is not even possible without reflection, be-

*From Jung, *Psychology and Religion*, originally published in English: The
Terry Lectures of 1937 at Yale University (1938), revised in accordance
with the Swiss edition (1940) in *The Collected Works of C. G. Jung*, Volume
11: *Psychology and Religion*, 2nd ed., paragraphs 2-5, 11, 14-16, 26, 36-37, 41.
Copyright ©1975 by Princeton University Press. Reprinted by permission
of Princeton University Press.

cause "experience" is a process of assimilation without which there could be no understanding. As this statement indicates, I approach psychological matters from a scientific and not from a philosophical standpoint. Inasmuch as religion has a very important psychological aspect, I deal with it from a purely empirical point of view, that is, I restrict myself to the observation of phenomena and I eschew any metaphysical or philosophical considerations. I do not deny the validity of these other considerations, but I cannot claim to be competent to apply them correctly.

I am aware that most people believe they know all there is to be known about psychology, because they think that psychology is nothing but what they know of themselves. But I am afraid psychology is a good deal more than that. While having little to do with philosophy, it has much to do with empirical facts, many of which are not easily accessible to the experience of the average man. It is my intention to give you a few glimpses of the way in which practical psychology comes up against the problem of religion. It is self-evident that the vastness of the problem requires far more than three lectures, as the necessary elaboration of concrete detail takes a great deal of time and explanation. My first lecture will be a sort of introduction to the problem of practical psychology and religion. The second is concerned with facts which demonstrate the existence of an authentic religious function in the unconscious. The third deals with the religious symbolism of unconscious processes.

Since I am going to present a rather unusual argument, I cannot assume that my audience will be fully acquainted with the methodological standpoint of the branch of psychology I represent. This standpoint is exclusively phenomenological, that is, it is concerned with occurrences, events, experiences–in a word, with facts. Its truth is a fact and not a judgment. When psychology speaks, for instance, of the motif of the virgin birth, it is only concerned with the fact that there is such an idea, but it is not concerned with the question whether such an idea is true or false in any other sense. The idea is psychologically true inasmuch as it exists. Psychological existence is subjective in so far as an idea occurs in only one individual. But it is objective in so far as that idea is shared by a society–by a *consensus gentium.*

This point of view is the same as that of natural science. Psychology deals with ideas and other mental contents as zoology, for instance, deals with the different species of animals. An elephant is "true" because it exists. The elephant is neither an inference nor a statement nor the subjective judgment of a creator. It is a phenomenon. But we are so used to the idea that psychic events are wilful and arbitrary products, or even the inventions of a human creator, that we can hardly rid ourselves of the prejudiced view that the psyche and its contents are nothing but our own arbitrary invention or the more or less illusory product of supposition and judgment. The fact is that certain ideas exist almost everywhere and at all times and can even spontaneously create themselves quite independently of migration and tradition. They are not made by the individual, they just happen to him—they even force themselves on his consciousness. This is not Platonic philosophy but empirical psychology. . . .

As I am a doctor and a specialist in nervous and mental diseases, my point of departure is not a creed but the psychology of the *homo religiosus*, that is, of the man who takes into account and carefully observes certain factors which influence him and his general condition. It is easy to designate and define these factors in accordance with historical tradition or ethnological knowledge, but to do the same thing from the standpoint of psychology is an uncommonly difficult task. What I can contribute to the question of religion is derived entirely from my practical experience, both with my patients and with so-called normal persons. As our experience with people depends to a large extent upon what we do with them, I can see no other way of proceeding than to give you at least a general idea of the line I take in my professional work. . . .

But what, actually, is the psyche? Materialistic prejudice explains it as a mere epiphenomenal by-product of organic processes in the brain. Any psychic disturbance must therefore be an organic or physical disorder which is undiscoverable only because of the inadequacy of our present methods of diagnosis. The undeniable connection between psyche and brain gives this point of view a certain weight, but not enough to make it an unshakable truth. We do not know whether there is a real disturbance of the organic processes in the brain in a case of neurosis, and if there are disorders of an endocrine nature it is impossible to say whether they might not be effects rather than causes.

On the other hand, it cannot be doubted that the real causes of neurosis are psychological. Not so long ago it was very difficult to imagine how an organic or physical disorder could be relieved by quite simple psychological means, yet in recent years medical science has recognized a whole class of diseases, the psychosomatic disorders, in which the patient's psychology plays the essential part. Since my readers may not be familiar with these medical facts I may instance a case of hysterical fever, with a temperature of 102°, which was cured in a few minutes through confession of the psychological cause. A patient with psoriasis extending over practically the whole body was told that I did not feel competent to treat his skin trouble, but that I should concentrate on his psychological conflicts, which were numerous. After six weeks of intense analysis and discussion of his purely psychological difficulties, there came about as an unexpected by-product the almost complete disappearance of the skin disease. In another case, the patient had recently undergone an operation for distention of the colon. Forty centimetres of it had been removed, but this was followed by another extraordinary distention. The patient was desperate and refused to permit a second operation, though the surgeon thought it vital. As soon as certain intimate psychological facts were discovered, the colon began to function normally again.

Such experiences make it exceedingly difficult to believe that the psyche is nothing, or that an imaginary fact is unreal. Only, it is not there where a near-sighted mind seeks it. It exists, but not in physical form. It is an almost absurd prejudice to suppose that existence can only be physical. As a matter of fact, the only form of existence of which we have immediate knowledge is psychic. We might well say, on the contrary, that physical existence is a mere inference, since we know of matter only in so far as we perceive psychic images mediated by the senses. . . .

As a matter of fact, it only needs a neurosis to conjure up a force that cannot be dealt with by rational means. Our cancer case [of a patient with an imaginary cancer] shows clearly how impotent man's reason and intellect are against the most palpable nonsense. I always advise my patients to take such obvious but invincible nonsense as the manifestation of a power and a meaning they have not yet understood. Experience has taught me that it is much more effective to take these things seriously and then look for a suitable explanation. But an explanation is suitable only when it produces a hypothesis equal to the morbid effect. Our patient is confronted with a power of will and suggestion more than equal to anything his consciousness can put against it. In this precarious situation it would be bad strategy to convince him that in some incomprehensible way he is at the back of his own symptom, secretly inventing and supporting it. Such a suggestion would instantly paralyse his fighting spirit, and he would get demoralized. It is far better for him to understand that his complex is an autonomous power directed against his conscious personality. Moreover, such an explanation fits the actual facts much better than a reduction to personal motives. An apparently personal motivation does exist, but it is not made by his will, it just happens to him. . . .

My patient is now very curious how I shall set about getting at the contents that form the root of the obsession. I then inform him, at the risk of shocking him severely, that his dreams will provide us with all the necessary information. We will take them as if they issued from an intelligent, purposive, and, as it were, personal source. This is of course a bold hypothesis and at the same time an adventure, because we are going to give extraordinary credit to a discredited entity–the psyche–whose very existence is still denied by not a few contemporary psychologists as well as by philosophers. . . .

Yet in dreams we find, without any profound analysis, the same conflicts and complexes whose existence can also be demonstrated by the association test. Moreover, these complexes form an integral part of the existing neurosis. We have, therefore, reason to believe that dreams can give us at least as much information as the association test can about the content of a neurosis. As a matter of fact, they give very much more. The symptom is like the shoot above ground, yet the main plant is an extended rhizome underground. The rhizome represents the content of a neurosis; it is the matrix of complexes, of symptoms, and of dreams. We have every reason to belief that dreams mirror exactly the underground processes of the psyche. And if we get there, we literally get at the "roots" of the disease. . . .

There are, as you know, numerous works on the phenomenology of dreams, but very few that deal with their psychology. This for the obvious reason that a psychological interpretation of dreams is an exceedingly ticklish and risky business. Freud has made a courageous attempt to elucidate the intricacies of dream psychology with the help of views which he gathered in the field of psychopathology. Much as I admire the boldness of his attempt, I cannot agree either with his method or with its results. He explains the dream as a mere façade behind which something has been carefully hidden. There is no doubt that neurotics hide disagreeable things, probably just as much as normal people do. But it is a serious question whether this category can be applied to such a normal and world-wide phenomenon as the dream. I doubt whether we can assume that a dream is something other than it appears to be. I am rather inclined to quote another Jewish authority, the Talmud, which says: "The dream is its own interpretation." In other words *I take the dream for what it is*. The dream is such a difficult and complicated thing that I do not dare to make any assumptions about its possible cunning or its tendency to deceive. The dream is a natural occurrence, and there is no earthly reason why we should assume that it is a crafty device to lead us astray. It occurs when consciousness and will are to a large extent extinguished. It seems to be a natural product which is also found in people who are not neurotic. Moreover, we know so little about the psychology of the dream process that we must be more than careful when we introduce into its explanation elements that are foreign to the dream itself.

2. Pro-Freudian View of Jung as Non-Empirical

Walter Kaufmann was well-known for his works on Nietzsche. He regarded Freud as a successor to Nietzsche. In the following selection he takes a pro-Freudian view on Jung. The selection is from his Discovering the Mind, *Volume 3:* Freud versus Adler and Jung *(1980). It represents a severe criticism of Jung by a well-known scholar.*

Jung, much more even than Adler, became a guru. Many of his patients did not have specific symptoms when they came to him but sought help in finding a meaning for their lives. And Jung himself stressed his eclecticism (16, 74f.). . . .

Among Jung's patients were wealthy American women [e.g., Mary Mellon], eager to do something for the cause. Eventually, the publication of his collected works, in English and German, was subsidized, and the volumes were produced very beautifully and underpriced, and then also made available in extremely attractive paperbacks. The Bollingen Series, established for this purpose, made room not only for Jung but also for a few other prestigious writers as well as a number of works dealing with Oriental religions, thus providing a very appealing setting for Jung. . . .

Jung makes no demands on us. He provides diversions and escapes. Readers who are aware of Jung's rebellion against Freud are only too ready to believe that Freud was an intolerant, dogmatic old

*From Walter Kaufmann, *Discovering the Mind*, Vol. 3: *Freud versus Adler and Jung* (New York: McGraw-Hill, 1980), pp. 397-398, 426-427, 429.

tyrant while Jung was a revolutionary. But Jung was an archetypal counterrevolutionary.

Freud's account of Jung in his *History* (cited in Section 58) was as perceptive as most of what Jung wrote on Freud is obtuse. Among the points one might add to it is that people prefer stories and fairy tales–soothing diversions–to austere challenges. . . .

In the end we shall also return to the beginning of these reflections on Jung. . . . Jung's first letter to Künzli, whom he wrote soon after how philosophy was a systemized fight against one's own insecurity, is an even more astonishing document. Arnold Künzli was a student who had said in a review of one of Jung's books in a student newspaper that "much in Jung is still the romantic vision of a creative spirit, occasionally at the expense of scientific empiricism." Although Künzli apparently had not said anything worse than that, Jung felt so piqued that he sent Künzli a long handwritten letter, February 4, 1943:. . . .

This extraordinary outburst shows how, so late in life, Jung was still fighting his own insecurity, seeking reassurance in his honorary degrees.

About the Harvard degree: The committee at Harvard had wanted to give Freud an honorary degree but was assured by Erik Erikson that there was no chance at all that Freud would accept. It was 1936, the year he turned eighty. Had their offer been rejected, the next offer would have been made by a different committee, and the psychologists wanted very much to honor a psychologist. So they offered the degree to Jung. . . .

Künzli had kindled Jung's wrath by questioning how scientific he was. It was terribly important to Jung to be considered no less scientific than Freud, if not more so, but at the same time not opposed to religion. Like Kant, Jung wanted to reconcile science and religion. And in Jung's case as in Kant's that, as much as anything, accounts for his wide appeal.

3. In Search of Jung

J. J. Clarke*

J. J. Clarke's In Search of Jung *(1992) provides a current perspective on the charges against Jung. As the title suggests, Jung's meanings were sometimes not easily discernible. Clarke enumerates the attacks against Jung's work. He goes on to give a spirited defense of Jung as empirical. Whether one fully agrees with him the following selection summarizes the charges and illustrates a defense.*

Jung once remarked that

> Because I am an empiricist first and foremost, and my views are grounded in experience, I had to deny myself the pleasure of reducing them to a well ordered system and of placing them in their historical and ideological context. From the philosophical standpoint, of whose requirements I am very well aware, this is indeed a painful omission.
>
> (CW18.1731)

It is unlikely that we would learn much from attempting to reduce his ideas to a 'well ordered system', and indeed Jung frequently expressed doubts about the desirability of any such task. On the other hand there is a great need to place his ideas 'in their historical and ideological context'. Despite ever-increasing fame, and an ever-growing band of devoted followers, both the public and the scholarly

---

*From J. J. Clarke, *In Search of Jung* (London and New York: Routledge, 1992), pp. xiii-xiv, 4, 9-11, 22, 35, 37-38, 74, 116, 128-129. Reprinted by permission.

perception of him is still largely that of a maverick and a 'mystic', something of a deviant who stands outside the mainstream of our culture. Jung himself foresaw this fate when, very late in his life, he lamented the widespread misunderstanding of his work which was, he believed, the result of being 'isolated between the faculties' (*Letters II*, p. 629).

The aim of this book is to help to release Jung from this isolation and to show that, even though he may fall between academic disciplines, he has an important and honoured place at the heart of the great debates of modern times. By contrast with Freud, Jung has not yet achieved the status which he deserves, and I believe that this must be rectified by reexamining the part he has played in the history of modern thought. Freud's place in our culture is secure. Though his ideas and theories have by no means received universal acclaim, and are the subject of continued controversy, his influence and status are assured and can be observed in a wide variety of fields ranging from philosophy and sociology to art and literary criticism. Jung, on the other hand, though founder of a worldwide therapeutic community, and despite a powerful impact on theology, and a high reputation amongst 'New Age' thinkers, has for the most part been looked upon with disfavour, and even with contempt, by the academic guardians of our culture. It is the aim of this book to show that Jung, as much as Freud, deserves a secure place in the history of ideas of the twentieth century, that he is not to be viewed as a minor act in the Freudian saga but as part of that great tradition of philosophical anthropology which, since Plato and Aristotle, has wrestled with the central issue of human nature and human destiny. . . .

. . . His influence is undoubtedly growing, though it remains largely unacknowledged, and he is still frequently consigned to neglect, or referred to in passing with a patronizing sneer.

Here are a few examples of what I mean. In a recent comprehensive survey of psychological theories Hearnshaw refers in a few rather grudging paragraphs on Jung to 'the strongly mystical strain in his outlook' and to his 'flirtations with alchemy, oriental cults and occultism' (1987, p. 166). Hughes in an important book on social criticism generously allows that 'it would be wrong to dismiss Jung as a charlatan', but goes on to aver that '[Jung's] mind was profoundly confused, and his writings are a trial to anyone who attempts to discover in them a logical sequence of ideas', and characterizes him as a 'mystagogue' parading in the guise of a man of science (1979, p.

160). In a similar vein, but more summarily, Peters, in his contribution to *Brett's History of Psychology*, dismisses Jung's work as 'so mysterious as to be almost undiscussable' (1962, p. 730), a remark which echoes Freud's own comment of 1914 that Jung's views were 'so obscure, unintelligible and confused as to make it difficult to take up any position upon (them)' (Freud 1914, p. 121). Rycroft is barely more charitable when he observes that he (Rycroft) 'suffers from the not uncommon constitutional defect of being incapable of understanding Jung's writings' (1972, p. ix). Fromm, a Freudian sympathizer, was a particularly trenchant critic of Jung, referring to him as 'a reactionary romantic', accusing him of lacking 'commitment and authenticity', and of replacing the search for truth with 'a seductive spirituality and brilliant obscurantism' (quoted in G. Wehr, 1987, p. 475). The 'official' Freudian view of Jung is expressed by Ernest Jones, Freud's disciple and biographer, who commented that after his early important studies in word-association techniques and in schizophrenia, Jung descended 'into pseudo-philosophy out of which he never emerged'. And perhaps most unfriendly of all was Glover's dismissal of Jung's work as 'a mishmash of oriental philosophy with bowdlerised psychology' (1950, p. 134). . . .

. . . He consistently refused right to the end of his life to give any place to metaphysical explanations in his formal psychological work. His interest in the occult, which was certainly lifelong, has frequently been cited in support of the appellation 'mystic', but this is to confuse the study of the occult as a psychological phenomenon with an active sympathy with and theoretical commitment to it. As Jung himself noted: 'If you call me an occultist because I am seriously investigating religious, mythological, and philosophical fantasies . . . then you are bound to diagnose Freud as a sexual pervert since he is doing likewise with sexual fantasies' (*Letters II*, p. 186). . . .

. . . in the crucial area of mythology it is clear that Jung took the lead, and indeed, in a rare moment of generosity towards his erstwhile colleague, Freud admitted that Jung was the first to draw attention to the striking similarity between the disordered fantasies of sufferers from schizophrenia and the myth of primitive peoples. It was in 1909 that Jung first disclosed his interest in the history of religion and mythology, declaring in a letter to Freud that 'mythology has got me in his grip', and urging his friend and colleague to 'cast a beam of light in that direction'. Freud's initial response was cool, and he warned Jung, prophetically as it turned out, that if he persisted he would be accused of 'mysticism', but he quickly warmed to the idea and wrote to Jung of his 'delight' that he was 'going into mythology' (McGuire, 1988, p. 260). It is true that Freud had already recognized the relevance of mythology to psychoanalytic investigation, but the letters indicate that it was Jung who was more acutely aware of the links between ancient myth and the modern psyche, who goaded him on to a deeper interest in the subject, and stimulated a competitive spirit between them.

. . . Philosophers of science nowadays make a distinction between the 'context of discovery' and the 'context of justification'. Thus, to take a familiar example, the insight into universal gravitation which inspired Newton as he sat in his garden at Woolsthorpe watching the applies fall needed the hard intellectual work of the *Principia* in order to transform it into a scientific law. Jung's own 'context of discovery' was the period of 'confrontation with the unconscious' which followed his break with Freud when powerful images and thoughts flooded in on him, and it required the mature reflection of a lifetime to transform the insights of this period into some sort of psychological theory. Intuition and imagination, then, though necessary, are not sufficient for knowledge, as he makes clear in the following passage written in his last years:

> The safe basis of real intellectual knowledge and moral understanding gets lost if one is content with the vague satisfaction of having understood by 'hunch'. One can explain and know only if one has reduced intuitions to an exact knowledge of facts and their logical connections.
>
> (MS, p. 82)

This point has important bearing on those critics of Jung, such as Philip Rieff, who are inclined to dismiss him as being more a religious seer than a scientist. 'Jung's was a language of faith', Rieff claims, 'revelatory, and therefore beyond the danger of being invalidated by argument or contradicted by experience', and concludes that 'Jung's theory amounts at once to a private religion and an anti-science' (1973, pp. 97-8). While it may be the case that Jung, like many great scientists, made his important discoveries in a context that transcends logic, his life was devoted to the hard intellectual work of testing out these discoveries through clinical and historical investigation. . . .

... Jung certainly took the experiences and beliefs associated with metaphysical and religious systems seriously; indeed a large part of his writings is devoted to the study of themes from Christian theology, alchemy, astrology, Gnosticism, Taoism, and yoga, and he devoted many years of work and considerable scholastic skill to an understanding of these beliefs. But his approach to these systems of thought was always explicitly *phenomenological*, and he was always careful to leave on one side as irrelevant to his enterprise the truth-claims contained in them. That is, his interest in, say, Christian beliefs lay, not in the question of whether they were true or false, a matter on which he pronounced himself officially agnostic, but rather in the role that they played within the psychic life of the individual or the group. . . .

Whatever the uncertainties and distortions that inevitably arise in studying the phenomena of consciousness, these remained, Jung believed, strictly *empirical* in nature. He frequently reiterated the claim that he was first and foremost an empiricist, and throughout his life stood by the belief that his study of the psyche was not philosophy but an empirical science. He himself was reared in an empiricist tradition, and the early development of his theories while at the Burghölzli Hospital, especially those connected with the idea of autonomous complexes, were entirely based on empirical research, some of it involving experiments that would not be out of place in a modern psychology laboratory.

Nevertheless his use of the term, as with the parallel term 'phenomenology', requires some explanation, especially in view of the fact that the phrase 'empirical psychology' has acquired a meaning quite distant from that which Jung used in reference to his own studies. Historically the issue was a pressing one for him in the light of the cultural hegemony in his lifetime of positivism, with its commitment to a fundamental empiricism. In addition to this broader consideration, Jung was in general very wary of *a priori* theorizing. This attitude no doubt had its foundation in his own personality with its powerful orientation towards personal experience, but it is also evident in his rejection of Freud's sexual theory which he came to see as the unwarranted imposition of theory upon evidence, and in his insistence as a therapist on treating the individual case rather than in attempting to apply general theories indiscriminately.

When we come to examine his theory of archetypes in Part II we will observe two sorts of empirical evidence adduced in support of the theory. The first is clearly *phenomenological* in the sense just discussed, namely the sort of information provided by patients in recounting dreams, fantasies, and so forth. For Jung psychic data such as dreams were regarded as empirical facts in the same way that natural scientists regarded specimens and instrument readings. Such data are no doubt subject to a variety of distortions, but as I have suggested Jung was fully aware of this; such distortions represent a congenital defect which, though rendering psychology a very imperfect science, does not alter in principle its empirical credentials. The second sort of evidence is *cultural*, namely the publicly observable and recordable activities of groups of people expressed in the form of myth, religion, art and literature. Thus Jung's study of alchemy is essentially empirical in the unexceptionable sense that it is based on a study of records of a specific class of cultural activity. In this sense Jung's work is no more nor less empirical than the work of ethnologists, anthropologists, historians and sociologists, and indeed draws on work from all these specialisms.

However, despite his oft-affirmed devotion to the 'phenomena', his claim to the title of 'empiricist', and his conscious tendency to want to avoid theoretical abstractions–'how difficult and thankless is the task of theory-building in psychology' (CW16.203)–Jung's writings do in fact display a marked inclination towards speculation and to the formulation of conjectures and hypotheses. It is important to see that this tendency in no way conflicted with his basic Kantian assumptions. In 1937 he noted that 'Although I have often been called a philosopher, I am an empiricist and adhere to the phenomenological standpoint'. But he immediately proceeded to qualify this remark in the following terms: 'I trust that it does not conflict with the principles of scientific empiricism if one occasionally makes certain reflections which go beyond a mere accumulation and classification of experience' (CW11.2), and elsewhere he remarked that 'science cannot exist without hypotheses' (CW10.1041). Thus his theory of archetypes, formulated shortly after his break with Freud, was by no means a mere 'accumulation and classification of experience', but was put forward as a bold and speculative hypothesis designed to explain a wide range of phenomena. This speculative spirit became even more marked in the later years of his life, following the Second World War and a critical illness, most obviously in his theory of *synchronicity*, the hypothesis that in addition to the principle of mechanical causation it was necessary to postulate a principle to explain meaningful coincidences. But even here the aim was to offer, not some metaphysical insight, but rather an explanatory hypothesis to explain certain observable phenomena. It is true that he was not prepared to accept the constraints of a materialist world-view, and thus to explain everything in terms of matter and physical energy, but this world-view itself, as we saw, was for him a metaphysical assumption rather than an unchallengeable truth. . . .

. . . His fascination with the world's religious and spiritual traditions, and the central role they played in his thinking, have caused confusion amongst his critics. On the one hand Erich Fromm contemptuously dismissed 'his blend of outmoded superstition, indeterminate heathen idol-worship, and vague talk about God' as representing 'exactly the right mix in an age which possesses but little faith and judgement' (quoted in G. Wehr, 1987, p. 475). By contrast Murray Stein sees Jung as attempting nothing less than a reconstruction of Christian theology (1985). And Colin Wilson, standing somewhere between these two extremes, believed that Jung was never actually the scientist he claimed to be, but was an occultist in disguise, and a 'guru of the Western world' (1984, p. 9). Jung himself was painfully aware of the confusion thus caused, and ruefully commented in 1952 that in his time he had been regarded 'not only as a Gnostic and its opposite, but also as a theist and an atheist, a mystic and a materialist', adding that he approved by contrast the opinion of the *British Medical Journal* that he was, as he had always claimed, 'an empiricist first and last' (CW18.1502). . . .

Jung's view of the collective unconscious is something of a scandal. While the idea that there is such a thing as an *individual* unconscious has, since Freud popularized this notion, become widely accepted, Jung's belief that there is another layer beneath the unconscious which in some way binds us to the whole of mankind seems to fly in the face of both common sense and conventional wisdom, to be 'mystically conceived', as Wilhelm Reich dismissively put it.

Since John Locke supposedly demolished the concept of innate ideas in the seventeenth century, it has become virtually a dogma of Western thought that the mind is furnished only with ideas which come through the senses during the lifetime of the individual. Even the mediaeval theologians had followed the Aristotelian dictum: *nihil in intellectu quod nisi prius in sensu*–anything in the intellect must first come from the senses. Any idea that the mind already has at birth a stock of knowledge, or that we inherit from our parents anything other than our physical constitution, smacks of metaphysics or, worse, of mysticism. This is linked with the widespread assumption amongst modern psychologists that all distinctively human behaviour is acquired through learning, and a parallel assumption of ethologists that human qualities are based on culture rather than genetic transmission.

In this chapter I want to show that Jung's views on the collective unconscious are neither metaphysical nor mystical and that, whether or not we accept them as true, they do represent a plausible hypothesis, and make an important contribution to contemporary debates on human behaviour and its evolution. . . .

Jung has often been accused of neglecting the biological and instinctual basis of the human personality, of showing, unlike Freud, comparatively little interest in the 'lower' functions of human life, especially the sexual instinct, and of propounding a purely spiritualistic psychology. In the previous chapter I argued that, contrary to this prejudice, Jung's theory of archetypes was premised on the belief that the symbolic life of the mind was firmly rooted in biology and instinct. Some critics such as Steele have argued, however, that this whole approach is a mistaken one and that Jung's rather sketchy attempts to link archetypal inheritance with biology is superfluous. Steele believes 'Jung's work does not require any natural scientific support', and that the strength of argument concerning archetypes lay in his *hermeneutical* approach which rests entirely on the language of meaning, and that any attempt to intrude the causal language of the biological sciences into this domain would involve a kind of category mistake (Steele, 1982, p. 331f. See also Neumann, 1954, for a similar view).

Furthermore, as Stevens points out, many recent followers of Jung have chosen to follow an 'esoteric path' which emphasizes the spiritual nature of the archetypes, and have been reluctant to 'elucidate the biological implications of Jung's theories', and in so doing have 'neglected the archetype's behavioural manifestations no less than its phylogenetic roots' (1982, p. 29). A tragic consequence of this, Stevens believes, has been a divorcing of analytical psychology from the mainstream of the behavioural sciences, and a confirmation in many people's minds of the supposed 'mystical' bent of Jung's thought.

I believe that the strength of Jung's whole approach lay in his attempt to integrate his theory of archetypes into a unified theory which embraced both the psychic and the biological realms, and hence that 'man must remain conscious of the world of the archetypes, because in it he is still a part of Nature and is connected with his own roots' (CW9i.174). According to Jung, as I interpret him, the human psyche is an integral part of the natural world and not an alien visitor to it. Body and mind constitute together a single whole, and hence the 'separation of psychology from the basic assumptions of biology is purely artificial, because the human psyche lives in indissoluble union with the body' (CW8.232).

4. Review of Richard Noll, *The Jung Cult*

Barbara Stephens*

Richard Noll's The Jung Cult: Origins of a Charismatic Movement *(Princeton, 1994) is a recent challenge to the view that Jung was empirical—and to the theory of the collective unconscious. Barbara Stephens reviewed it in* Psychological Perspectives *(Spring-Summer 1995). An analytical psychologist, she provides an assessment of the strengths and weaknesses of the work. The journal* Psychological Perspectives *is published semi-annually by the C. G. Jung Institute of Los Angeles.*

Richard Noll has formulated a hypothesis which, in itself, is quite provocative. He claims that analytic psychology is not a psychology at all, but a religious movement that has all the trappings of a cult. Like any cult, its founder has been divinized, his writing sacralized, his followers categorized into castes of priests (Jungian analysts), disciples (analysands, clients, and other student types) and various New Age groupies. The operation of the Jung cult is structured, he claims, "like a multi-level marketing pyramid, with individuation as the vague product sold and . . . money, perceived power, and perceived spirituality all flow[ing] to the few certified Jungian analysts in the elite at the top in this pyramidal economic system, who essentially buy their 'distributorship.'" Stripped to its core, this is not a new hypothesis. The entire "psychoanalytic movement" has been

*From Barbara Stephens, review of *The Jung Cult* by Richard Noll, *Psychological Perspectives*, Issue 31 (Spring-Summer 1995), pp. 142-145. Reprinted with permission from *Psychological Perspectives*, Issue 31, ©1995 by the C. G. Jung Institute of Los Angeles, CA 90064 (10349 W. Pico Blvd., Los Angeles, CA 90064).

wrapped in a non-scientific cloak since its turn-of-the-century inception, despite the efforts and disclaimers of its advocates. It's not even new to see the Jungian path of the psychoanalytic road labeled "religious." What is new is the context of scholarship into which this hypothesis is imbedded. And it *is* scholarship.

Dr. Noll, a clinical psychologist and post-doctoral Fellow in the History of Science at Harvard University, takes us through a well-referenced historical analysis of six of Jung's interconnected theories: complexes, psychological types, phylogenetic unconscious, collective unconscious, archetypes, and the principle of individuation. As an historian, Dr. Noll is looking for the ideational birthplace of Jung's theories and listening for the intellectual reverberations of earlier thinkers. He finds them buried in the not-so-shallow grave of the German *"völkisch"* movement of the 18th and 19th centuries, with its accompanying neopaganisms, nature philosophies, mythologies, and mystery cults. As he digs up the ground and quotes from the unearthed texts, names unfamiliar to most psychologists or relegated to referenced citations (such as Ernst Haeckels, Frederick Max Müller, Eugen Diederick, Johann Jacob Bachofen, Frederick Cruezer), begin to sound strikingly "Jungian"–which is, after all, one of Dr. Noll's points. Scintillating and juicy historical tidbits also emerge as he burrows along: August Strindberg reveling in ancient pagan rites in a Hungarian castle; Otto Gross' all-night analytic sessions in Schwabing cafes; Leonhard Seif, Emma Jung's first psychoanalyst, disclosing details of her sessions to Ernst [sic] Jones, who relayed them to Freud; case notes of Hermann Hesse's analytic sessions; Jung, deleting citations of his students' scholarship. It is hard to image anyone interested in the evolution of ideas unimpressed by this historical archeology of Jung's intellectual ancestry.

As impressive as I found Dr. Noll's work historically, I found it progressively more suspect philosophically. It is, in my opinion, a philosophical nightmare!

My argument is not with the historical data Dr. Noll presents, but with his style of presentation, his method of argumentation, and his conclusions. How you present material is often critical to the conclusion you want the reader to make, consciously or otherwise. The same piece of courtroom evidence, for example, is presented quite differently by the prosecution than by the defense. Moreover, as every analyst knows, the goals, motivations, and valuations of the presenter, veiled by content, can often be exposed by the manner of presentation, or, at least, suggested. Dr. Noll's historical scholarship veils a style of argumentation and rhetoric that leads a reader directly toward conclusions that, at best, caricature analytic psychology and its adherents.

Noll's book is liberally sprinkled with such taboos of logic as gratuitous assumptions, unsubstantiated claims, inflated language, and causal inferences based on comparative associations. Often the content is so historically engaging, it's hard to see the logical mishaps clearly. For example, Dr. Noll traces the development of the current analytic psychology clubs back to 1912 and the Society for Psychoanalytic Endeavors. Members were those

> . . . rare Europeans who had sought out the modern and controversial treatment of psychoanalysis for their problems and found great meaning in its view of human nature. They . . . submitted themselves to a form of treatment in which intimate sexual details of their lives were freely handed over to others. Such intimate self-disclosure proved to be a powerful act of liberation, while facilitating one's bonding to a new group of like-minded people. The most intimate sexual activities were then discussed in graphic terminology with other patients . . . .

Wait! No substantive evidence is provided for the last sentence, either in footnotes or the body of the text. We are simply being carried along toward an unsubstantiated generic conclusion by inference. The syllogism might go like this: Patients reveal intimate sexual details to their analysts. They feel liberated and join a "like-minded" group. *Therefore,* they share intimate sexual details with other club members. Structured in its logical form, the error is clear and blatant. Dr. Noll, however, is spared having to state the inferred conclusion directly. His rhetoric and thematic associations simply lead the reader into it. This is only one out of many similarly structured errors in reasoning in this book. Often, it seemed as if the presentation of historical data provided a smokescreen for faulty argumentation, which, in this case, casts an unsavory and unwarranted shadow on the internal affairs of *any* analytic psychology club, past or present. Here again we get a *caricature,* not an accurate representation.

One of the more insidious conclusions a reader could make with this sort of argumentation is the comparison of Jungian theory and practice to national socialism and its cultist off-spring, Nazism. After all, as Dr. Noll carefully documents, both share many of the same *"völkisch"* intellectual ancestors. This is like suggesting that being influenced by Marxian themes constitutes a communist affiliation. On the book's jacket is the claim that "Noll firmly separates Jung and his teachings from the later National Socialist movement." I found this statement quite unconvincing, especially when I encountered such phases as "Jung's *Bund*" in reference to Jung's early supporters. This kind of inflammatory language peppers the book. It is flagrant journalistic "spin," not dispassionate scholarship. . . .

What I find most disappointing about *The Jung Cult* is that Dr. Noll's rhetoric may prevent those people most knowledgeable about Jungian theory and practice from taking the subject matter of his work seriously. His language almost guarantees an initial round of useless defensive posturing from supporters. Analytic psychology takes the spiritual and the sacred seriously in its clinical practice. This is not territory that can be easily described by using traditional psychological or psychoanalytic language. Whenever a path toward the sacred begins to open up, "groupies," devotees, and hero-worshippers sniff it out and prepare to trade potential individuation for its "feel-good" illusion. Does this make the Jungian community more susceptible to cultism? Does dedication to the spiritual dimension of human life constitute a *religion*? And if so, *so what*? How does a collective (institution, group, etc.) deal with the eruption of shadow material? The entire psychological community might benefit from a serious consideration of these and other questions prompted by the publication of *The Jung Cult*–which may be its most important contribution.

III. Was Jung Anti-Nazi or, for a Time, "a Nazi Sympathizer"?

1. Editorial (1933)

C. G. Jung*

Jung has had his detractors who were certain that he was "a Nazi sympathizer" and his admirers who were equally sure that he had always been anti-Nazi. Is the answer that simple? Or is the matter more complex? After the Nazis came to power in Germany in 1933, Ernst Kretschmer resigned as president of the General Medical Society for Psychotherapy in April to return to a position at the University of Marburg. Jung, who was vice president, succeeded him as president and as editor of the Society's journal. In December 1933 Jung published a somewhat ambiguously worded editorial in the journal. He might have worded it ambiguously with one eye to Nazi readers and the other eye to his own meaning. It gave rise to charges. A translation follows.

*From Jung, "Editorial (1933)," published in the *Zentralblatt für Psychotherapie und ihre Grenzgebiete* (Leipzig), VI:3 (December 1933), pp. 139-140, trans. and published in Jung, *Civilization in Transition*, Vol. 10 of *The Collected Works of C. G. Jung*, 2nd ed., paragraphs 1014-1015. Copyright ©1975 by Princeton University Press. Reprinted by permission of Princeton University Press.

Owing to the resignation of Professor Kretschmer, the president of the General Medical Society for Psychotherapy, the presidency and with it the administration of the *Zentralblatt für Psychotherapie* have fallen to me. This change coincided with the great political upheaval in Germany. Although as a science psychotherapy has nothing to do with politics, fate has willed it that I should take over the editorship of the *Zentralblatt* at a moment when the state of affairs in psychotherapy is marked by a confusion of doctrines and views not unlike the previous state of affairs in politics. One-sided and mutually exclusive methods of observation have exerted too far-reaching an influence not only on specialized medical opinion but also on the psychological views of many educated laymen. The resulting contradictions have only been sharpened by the spread of my own–very different–ideas, so that we can well speak of confusion being worse confounded. It will therefore be the primary task of the *Zentralblatt* to give impartial appreciation to all objective contributions, and to promote an over-all view which will do greater justice to the basic facts of the human psyche than has been the case up till now. The differences which actually do exist between Germanic and Jewish psychology and which have long been known to every intelligent person are no longer to be glossed over, and this can only be beneficial to science. In psychology more than in any other science there is a "personal equation," disregard of which falsifies the practical and theoretical findings. At the same time I should like to state expressly that this implies no depreciation of Semitic psychology, any more than it is a depreciation of the Chinese to speak of the peculiar psychology of the Oriental.

Psychotherapy has long ceased to be an exclusive province for specialists. The interest of the whole world is directed upon the psychological discoveries of medical men. Psychotherapy will therefore be obliged to take the whole of the psyche into account when constructing its theories, and to extend its vision beyond the merely pathological and personal. The efforts of the *Zentralblatt* will be directed to this end.

C. G. Jung

2. On Jung and Psychotherapy in Germany, 1933-1940

Geoffrey Cocks*

After the publication of Jung's editorial in the Zentralblatt *and a subsequent exchange with Dr. Gustav Bally in the* Neue Zürcher Zeitung *charges began to arise that Jung was a Nazi sympathizer and anti-Semitic. Geoffrey Cocks has investigated the matter of Jung and psychotherapy in Germany from 1933 to 1940. The following selection is from his* Psychotherapy in the Third Reich, *2nd edition (New Brunswick, NJ, forthcoming).*

What Jung hoped was to make the old society [General Medical Society for Psychotherapy] formally international in nature and thus to protect psychotherapy, including of course the Jungian variety, from extinction in Germany. In the best of all possible German worlds, survival might even lead to the unification of the various schools of thought, thus subordinating the powerful and autonomous psychoanalytic movement to a more comprehensive psychotherapy more amenable to the Jungian point of view. . . .

The International General Medical Society for Psychotherapy was headquartered in Zurich. Jung held a three-year term as president of the international society as well as heading the Swiss group which came into existence in 1935. The statutes of the international society were adopted at the seventh congress of the old General Medical Society at Bad Nauheim on May 15, 1934. As we have seen, these statutes attempted to counter the overwhelming weight of the German society: at the Bad Nauheim congress there were seventy-one German participants, two from Holland, a Swede, and a Swiss (Jung). On January 22, 1934, Jung had written to Poul Bjerre, who would become leader of a Swedish section of the international society in 1936, expressing his concern over just such an imbalance of power.

Jung also claimed to be acting in the interests of the Jewish members of the international society. When Max Guggenheim of Lausanne objected to Jung's role in working with the psychotherapists in Germany, Jung responded that, among other things, he had enabled [Rudolf] Allers, a Jew, to stay on as editor of the review section of the *Zentralblatt*. Jung also inserted a circular letter in the December 1934 issue of the *Zentralblatt* which declared that the "international society is neutral as to politics and creed." This separated membership in the international society from membership in any of the national groups within it, thus allowing German Jewish doctors to join the international society on an individual basis. But, as we have already seen, Jews could still be members of the German General Medical Society until 1938, when Jewish doctors lost the right to practice in Germany. . . .

In a letter to Alphonse Maeder of Zurich on January 22, 1934, Jung wrote that [former president] Kretschmer had stepped down because matters had become too complicated and that he, Jung, would not have accepted presidency of the General Medical Society for Psychotherapy had it not been for the insistence of the Germans that no German could effectively assume a post in an international organization under the prevailing conditions in Germany. There is no evidence that Jung forced Kretschmer's resignation in order to further his own designs and in his autobiography Kretschmer expresses no animus toward Jung. The German psychotherapists' preference was determined not only by their desire for the protection they believed Jung's worldwide reputation would provide, but also by Jung's great popularity and respect among proponents of a new German psychotherapy that was ferociously opposed to Freudian theories. Thus the genuine and justified anxiety that prompted German psychotherapists to engage Jung and motivated him to become involved in German affairs at this time also served for both as a cover for concession to, and enthusiasm for, National Socialism. Moreover, the Germans' use of Jung was also in his interest in promoting analytical psychology, particularly at the expense of its archival, Freudian psychoanalysis. . . .

Jung's motives for his actions between 1933 and 1940 have been widely questioned and attacked. It is true that most of his protests about the course of events in Germany went exclusively into the ears and eyes of non-Germans, but perhaps this was only prudent given the German environment. And even though Jung corresponded with [Kurt] Gauger concerning the protection that the eager professional parvenu and party man might be able to provide for psychotherapy, he professed to be aghast at Gauger's book on "political medicine." In 1935 he declared himself against naming Gauger as managing director of the German society, preferring, not unselfishly, his follower Curtius. Jung never became directly involved in the operations of the German General Medical Society [headed by Matthias Heinrich Göring] or of the Göring Institute. Even his role in the protection of psychotherapy was ambiguous in effect. His claim to have succeeded in "tucking away Psychotherapy in a remote department where the medical Nazi boss could not reach it" is inaccurate. Apart from the fact that Nazified state institutions were successfully fighting off party challenges, the equation of party with threat and state with opportunity (or at least protection) is far too simple a formulation. The Nazi preference for mobilization over reform, coupled with the conservative nationalism and Romantic medical orientation shared by party health ideologues and by most of German psychotherapists, made the party far less of a threat than it might have appeared at the time. And, as we have seen already, Göring was the key player in these machinations, not Jung.

The starting point for criticism of Jung is the introduction he contributed to the resuscitated *Zentralblatt* of December 1933. There he wrote that, in his capacity as editor, he saw his purpose as the clarification of various teachings, theories, and practices within a political context even though psychotherapy itself had nothing to do with politics. Jung's ambiguous embracing of forces, symbols, races, and elites led to the same sort of relativism that had paralyzed German intellectuals of the nineteenth and twentieth centuries. . . . In the same manner, in his introduction to the *Zentralblatt*, Jung found a formulation that fit both his own anthropological tendency toward national and racial characterization as well as the practical demands of the moment: "Genuinely independent and perceptive people have for a long time recognized that the difference between Germanic and Jewish psychology should no longer be effaced, something that can only be beneficial to the science."

Jung's words, and the fact that they were published alongside Göring's call to the Nazi colors, caused an international furor. Jung later claimed that Göring's essay was to have been published only in the special German supplement to the *Zentralblatt* and that it was only by accident that it had appeared in the "international" journal. Perhaps Jung was thinking of what was to become "Die nationalsozialistische Idee in der Psychotherapie," Göring's introductory essay to *Deutsche Seelenheilkunde,* and did not anticipate the strident pro-Nazi rhetoric of Göring's little communication, but surely he should have been–and probably was–aware that his remarks would be placed within a framework of loyalty to the Nazi cause in a journal that, while under Jung's editorship, was published and printed in Germany as the main public vehicle for the German psychotherapists. This was especially so in light of his German colleagues' efforts to associate his name, person, and theory with themselves.

Regardless of their context, however, Jung's observations were objectionable in and of themselves to many, as they seemed to support the official anti-Semitism of the Nazi government. In February 1934, Gustav Bally, a former Berlin psychoanalyst who had been forced to emigrate to Switzerland because of "anti-state activities," attacked Jung's future credibility as editor of a periodical subservient to the Nazi regime. Bally pointed to what he considered the damning emphasis Jung had placed on the supposed distinctions between Jewish and Germanic science, a common theme among Nazi intellectual apologists. At best, Bally concluded, Jung was unwittingly abetting National Socialism. One result of Bally's criticism was Göring's assurance to the Nazi party's Hermann Griesbeck that "my deputy" Kurt Gauger would look into the finances and by-laws of the Psychoanalytic Institute in Berlin. For his part, Jung replied to Bally by citing his "disappointment" at the publication of the Göring pledge of allegiance to Hitler in the *Zentralblatt* and by noting that he was president not of the German society but of the international society. Furthermore, Jung cautioned,

[a]s conditions then were, a single stroke of the pen in high places would have sufficed to sweep all psychotherapy under the table. That had to be prevented at all costs for the sake of suffering humanity, doctors and . . . science and civilization.

Jung's use of the past tense in 1934 is indicative of how his perception of the danger to psychotherapy had changed. This could evidence rueful reappraisal on the basis of a guilty conscience and/or an honest sense of having accomplished something positive in terms of the protection of psychotherapy. It is also an indication of the growing security won by the psychotherapists, a security Jung was probably trying to enhance by making a public distinction between "then" and "now." This would not only justify, to himself at least, his ongoing involvement with affairs in Germany, but also the policy adopted by the psychotherapists under Göring.

In response to Bally's objection to his distinction between German and Jew, Jung denied that he was making any value judgments and rejected the assertion that he had only recently and strategically begun emphasizing racial and cultural differences among peoples. It is clear in this instance, however, that he was attempting to use his own particular psychological view, with its criticism of the materialism of Freud's perspective and the rootlessness of modern Jewish culture, to protect psychotherapists in Germany. In an essay in the *Zentralblatt* in 1934, Jung again sought to distinguish between the Jewish and the "Aryan" unconscious, claiming that Freud "did not know the German soul, and neither do any of his blind adherents. Has not the shattering advent of National Socialism, upon which the world gazes with astonished eyes, taught them better?" . . .

On the other hand, by 1936 Jung was contemplating National Socialism in general with a more critical eye:

> The impressive thing about the German phenomenon is that one man, who is obviously 'possessed,' has infected a whole nation to such an extent that everything is set in motion and has started rolling on its course to perdition.

These words are from Jung's essay "Wotan," which Göring Institute Jungian Lucy Heyer-Grote claimed to have used in psychotherapy with comforting effect on patients who were opponents of the Nazi regime. It was a work that anticipated Jung's September 1939 judgment that "Hitler is reaching his climax and with him the German psychosis." In the realm of psychotherapy itself, earlier that same year Jung himself turned down a request from the editor of the *Zeitschrift für Rassenkunde*, Egon Freiherr von Eickstedt of Berlin, to write an article on contemporary racial problems. Two years before, Jung had been appalled to learn from C. A. Meier, managing editor of the *Zentralblatt*, that Göring had written for publication there a short review of official Nazi party philosopher Alfred Rosenberg's *Der Mythus des 20. Jahrhunderts* (1930). In a letter to Göring of November 16, Jung suggested that the book be passed over in silence and in fact the review did not appear, perhaps a sign that Jung and Meier could exercise some influence over what appeared in the journal's pages.

Jung's role in the affairs of psychotherapy in Germany diminished significantly once the German psychotherapists established their institute in May 1936. His major preoccupation from 1936 to 1940, when he resigned as president of the International General Medical Society, was with the international congresses and the controversies surrounding them. The controversies mostly had to do with the attempts of the Germans to assert their numerical dominance within the international society. . . .

. . . It must be said that Jung broke from . . . [anti-Semitic] notions in a way that suggests a dialectic of prejudice and tolerance within him that was ultimately resolved in favor of the latter. This is not to agree, however, with the argument of Wolfgang Giegerich that all along Jung was purposefully engaging the shadow of racial prejudice in order to extirpate it. Such a judgment naively ignores the plurality of motives and conditions present in any human action, a number of which we have explored in the case at hand. Such a rationalization also turns a blind eye to the negative effects of Jung's lack of vigorous early criticism of Hitler and the possible legitimacy for the regime created in the minds of many or some through Jung's association with it, whatever protective professional capacity he effected or intended.

3. New Material Regarding Jung, Anti-Semitism, and the Nazis

Jung to Mary Mellon, September 24, 1945:*

Recently some new material concerning Jung, anti-Semitism, and the Nazis has been discovered. Jung's letter to Mary Mellon, September 24, 1945–along with some other new material–was first published by Andrew Samuels (1993). Meanwhile, through my own research on Jung's friendship with Mary Mellon, I found that Jung had been the subject of an FBI investigation in 1944 into allegations that he was pro-Nazi and anti-Semitic. Interviewed by an FBI agent, Eleanor Bertine, a leading Jungian analyst in New York City, so informed Jung in December 1944. In the following extract from Jung's letter to Mary Mellon, friend, former patient, and editor of the Bollingen Series, Jung denies that he was ever a Nazi, but his letter leaves the charge of anti-Semitism open.

The war proved to be a great trial to me. People in the army were much better off. They could do something. I only could seek a refuge for my daughter-in-law, who was in the 8th month, and for my grandchildren in the western part of the Alps. That was in the blackest days of May 1940, when France broke down. On account of my critique of the German tyranny I was on the black list of the Gestapo, and if the Germans had invaded Switzerland, I would

---

*Jung to Mary Mellon, September 24, 1945, quoted in William Schoenl, *C. G. Jung: His Friendships with Mary Mellon and J. B. Priestley* (Wilmette, Ill.: Chiron Publications, forthcoming). Reprinted by permission of Niedieck Linder AG, literary agency for the Jung heirs.

certainly have been put on the spot. Well informed Germans told me so. My pupils in Germany were forced to repudiate my views publicly. I tell you these things, because you probably have heard the absurd rumor that I am a Nazi. This rumor has been started by the Freudian Jews in America. Their hatred of myself went as far as India, where I found falsified photo's [sic] of mine in the Psychological Seminar of Calcutta University. It was a photo retouched in such a way as to make me appear as an ugly Jew with a pince-nez! These photo's came from Vienna! This rumor has been spread over the whole world. Even with us it has been picked up with such alacrity, that I am forced to publish all the things I have written about Germany. It is however difficult to mention the antichristianism of the Jews after the horrible things that have happened in Germany. But Jews are not so damned innocent after all–the rôle played by the intellectual Jews in prewar Germany would be an interesting object of investigation. I have challenged the Nazis already in 1934 at a great reception in Frankfort in the house of Baron von Schnitzler, the Director of the I. G. Farben concern. I told them, that their anticlockwise Swastika is whirling down into the abyss of unconsciousness and evil. And this prediction has come off "and how"! After all this you can imagine our inexpressible joy, when we heard, that the Americans had gone ashore in Morocco!

4. Lingering Shadows: Jungians, Freudians and Anti-Semitism

Aryeh Maidenbaum*

The matter of anti-Semitism has cast a shadow over relations between Jungians and Freudians virtually since the break with Freud and, especially, since the time of Nazi Germany. Aryeh Maidenbaum and Stephen Martin brought together many of the views that have been expressed on this matter in their Lingering Shadows: Jungians, Freudians, and Anti-Semitism *(1991). In the Preface from which the following selection is taken, Maidenbaum tells how as a student at the Hebrew University he wanted to study analytical psychology at the C. G. Jung Institute of Zurich. There he and Martin became interested in the question whether Jung was anti-Semitic. Subsequently their interest evolved into* Lingering Shadows. *Maidenbaum concludes that Jung "was neither guilty of most of the accusations hurled at him nor wholly innocent of prejudice."*

The seed for this book was planted in Jerusalem, germinated in Zurich, and blossomed in New York. Some fifteen years ago, while applying for a postdoctoral grant from the Hebrew University to study at the C. G. Jung Institute in Switzerland, I was unexpectedly confronted with what I have now come to understand is the shadowy specter of Jung's "Jewish connection." Basically, I was told that Jung

*From *Lingering Shadows: Jungians, Freudians, and Anti-Semitism*, edited by Aryeh Maidenbaum & Stephen A. Martin. Reprinted by arrangement with Shambhala Publications, Inc., 300 Massachusetts Avenue, Boston, MA 02115.

was an anti-Semite at best and in fact quite possibly a Nazi sympathizer if not an active party member.

At the time, I was in analysis with Rivkah Schaerf Kluger, who then lived in Haifa, Israel. Dr. Kluger, a widely respected scholar and author, had been a student and analysand of Jung himself. Through her testimony, and the corroboration of other professors at the Hebrew University who had known Jung, I was able to rebut these accusations and convince both myself and university officials that the charges were unjust. I was ultimately granted the award and spent the next three years studying at the C. G. Jung Institute of Zurich.

Nevertheless, during my years of study and training, I began reading some of Jung's statements and became increasingly uncomfortable with my own ignorance of the topic. Moreover, Jung's public and private comments left me feeling that there was more to this topic than meets the eye. Realizing that the help I'd received personally from my Jungian analysis with Rivkah, combined with a passionate desire to train as a Jungian analyst, had propelled me to plow ahead as if caught in an archetypal force, I resolved to continue researching this topic until I felt satisfied I had all the facts straight. A fellow student and friend, Stephen Martin, shared my concern and curiosity, and we spent many an hour in Zurich discussing various aspects of Jung's work, his personal life history, and his attitudes toward and involvements with Jews during the 1930s and later. Helpful to us was the contact we had with individuals who had known Jung personally as well as the published and archival material available in Zurich.

Over the course of time, both Dr. Martin and I completed our studies, returned to the United States, established analytical practices, and became actively involved at the C. G. Jung Foundation of New York. What struck us both was that the subject of Jung and anti-Semitism kept cropping up over and over. We found, for example, that many of our non-Jungian professional colleagues who knew little or nothing about Jung and his work cited as a reason (thereby dismissing his unique contributions) the charge that he was a Nazi or an anti-Semite. Among the public at large, especially the academic world, many found their genuine interest in Jung's psychology and ideas threatened by accusations revolving around Jung's alleged anti-Semitism.

Over the years, Dr. Martin and I came to realize that while rebuttals have been written by Jungians themselves addressing this issue, there has been no systematic effort to examine it in an objective, scholarly, and balanced manner. The literature on this topic ranges from idolatry to witch hunting, from those who felt Jung could do no wrong to others who blatantly condemned him without familiarizing themselves with the factual material.

Dr. Martin and I spent several years organizing and gathering material for a conference that was held in the spring of 1989 on this topic. Our intent was to examine as much of the relevant data as was available and invite serious academicians as well as Jungian and non-Jungian analysts to objectively discuss the issue and its implications. The ultimate aim was to publish this resource book, encompassing all of Jung's pertinent statements on the topic and including several of the earlier pieces and the best of the conference material. We are pleased and gratified, both personally and on behalf of the conference sponsors, that we were able to accomplish this task. Moreover, as an added and unexpected bonus, we are most heartened that as a result of the interest generated by the New York conference, the International Association for Analytical Psychology added a special workshop on this topic at its August 1989 Conference in Paris. Presentations at that workshop are included in this volume. In addition, a bibliographical essay has been contributed by Jay Sherry to help direct serious students of the topic to all significant published material on this issue.

. . . The Board of the Jung Foundation [of New York], especially, is to be commended for its courage in facing this provocative question head on. The Board members were not only confident in Jung's unquestionably close personal connections with many of his leading Jewish students, but were also truly understanding that it was time for the important message inherent in Jung's psychology and ideas to stop being obscured by the controversy surrounding his life history. In this regard, we ourselves are convinced that Jung would have been the first to acknowledge that the message is more important than the messenger.

In examining the subject of both Jung's psychology and his life, the title *Lingering Shadows* seemed to leap out at us. There is apparently an inherently shadowy, perhaps unconscious area where many Jungians and Freudians meet in resisting further exploration of this topic. In Jungian terms we might say that the collective shadow of Jung's followers lay in zealously protecting the man and his public image for fear of uncovering some faults. Alternatively, it has become clear to us over the years that to this day the Freudian shadow, if you will, consists in keeping the emphasis on Jung the man while just as zealously resisting the importance of his psychology and ideas. Thus, unfortunately, in academic and analytical institutions around the country, it is remarkable how little attention is given to Jung's contributions to the field of depth psychology. Literally thousands of Ph.D.'s in psychology, M.S.W.'s, psychiatrists, and others in the helping professions receive their degrees each year with little or no knowledge of Jung's psychology and ideas.

It is Dr. Martin's and my hope that with the publication of *Lingering Shadows*, the public at large–lay and professional–will come to understand that Jung's approach to the psyche is the real under-lying, neglected issue. That Jung as a man had his strengths and weaknesses, his light and shadow, is a fact he himself would have been the first to admit. Jung often pointed out that great lights have great shadows. Carl Gustav Jung, being one of the most important figures in the development of the field of psychology, had both. In the end, when one goes to the trouble of sifting out all the material at hand, one comes to realize that he was neither guilty of most of the accusations hurled at him nor wholly innocent of prejudice, especially so in the early stages of his career. We trust and hope that this book will contribute to the important task at hand, that of lifting Jung's important message from the shadowy place to which it has been rele-gated and casting light on the many insights he has given us into the human psyche.

5. The Political Psyche

Andrew Samuels*

More than anyone else, Andrew Samuels has continued the investigation into the questions: Was Jung anti-Semitic and, for a time, "a Nazi sympathizer"? He has also discovered some new materials. He has brought his views together in two chapters of his recent book, The Political Psyche *(1993), from which the following selection is taken. Whether one agrees with all of his assessments or not he has brought forth work that cannot be ignored.*

In this chapter and the next one, I try to show that it was Jung's attempt to establish a psychology of nations that brought him into the same frame as Nazi anti-semitic ideology. In addition, Jung was absorbed by the question of leadership. Exploring these ideas as thoroughly as possible leads to a re-evaluation in more positive terms of what Jung was trying to do. Moreover, such an exploration is itself a necessary act of reparation. . . .

My own experience, as an analytical psychologist interested in relating Jung's work and legacy to that of psychoanalytic thinkers, is that relations between Freudians and Jungians are increasingly hampered by the repeated claims that Jung was a Nazi sympathizer and anti-semite. In 1987, I presented a clinical paper to a study group of the New York Psychoanalytic Institute. The first question concerned Jung's supposed 'admiration of Hitler' (in the questioner's words). I

---

*From Andrew Samuels, *The Political Psyche* (London and New York: Routledge, 1993), pp. 287-292, 294, 298-300, 307-311, 313-315, 320-325. Reprinted by permission.

had already noted that the entire audience on that occasion was, or seemed to be, Jewish, a fact which had produced in me a feeling of at-homeness up to the moment of that question. . . .

. . . There is very little critical work on the relationship of what is politically dubious in Jung's writings to the general cultural problems of Nazism and anti-semitism.

So, rather than attempt a new analysis of Jung the man (for which, not having met him, I feel I have not the slightest evidential basis), I sought a new use of what I had read. In these chapters, I ask whether there is something in the fundamental structure of Jung's thinking about the Jews, in its heart or essence, that made anti-semitism inevitable. When Jung writes about the Jews and Jewish psychology, is there something in his whole attitude that brings him into the same frame as the Nazis, even if he were shown not to have been an active Nazi collaborator? Is there something to worry about?

My brief answer, in distinction to that of many well-known Jungians, is 'yes' and, as I said, my hope is that by exploring the matter as deeply as I can a kind of reparation will ensue. Then there will be the base from which to explore the full potential of what Jung was trying to do with his psychological thinking about culture in the 1930s. . . .

. . . I believe that the manifold strengths and subtleties of analytical psychology are being lost. Such loss results, not only from the alleged Nazi collaboration and anti-semitism (both of which Jung denied), but also from what can sometimes seem like an inability on the part of many Jungians to react to such charges in an intelligent, humane and honest way. Thus, psychoanalysis and other intellectual disciplines are permitted to continue to ignore the pioneering nature of Jung's contributions and, hence, the work of post-Jungian analytical psychologists. . . .

Although what I write is primarily psychological, ideological and critical–not historical–it may help to provide some background information, which I will discuss throughout the chapters, for those not familiar with Jung's activities in the 1930s. I will also try to summarize, but not at this point critique, some of his ideas about 'Jewish psychology'. These activities and ideas have been the subject of intense argument from the 1930s to the present day. It has to be said that a definitive factual basis for clear-cut opinion is extremely difficult, if not impossible to establish. Nevertheless, when lecturing on the topic of Jung, anti-semitism and the Nazis, I have found widespread ignorance, even among Jungian analysts, of what it was that Jung did and said that has caused such a prolonged outcry. Non-Jungian audiences, on the other hand, have often seemed to 'know' definitely that Jung was 'anti-semitic', a 'supporter of Hitler', and so on–but not to be aware of the details.

In 1933 Jung took on the presidency of the General Medical Society for Psychotherapy. This was a professional body with members from several countries but nevertheless based in Germany and coming under Nazi control. Jung claimed that he took this post expressly to defend the rights of Jewish psychotherapists and he altered the constitution of the GSMP so that it became a fully and formally international (later, 'supranational') body. The former General Society became the German national member group. Membership was by means of national societies with a special category of individual membership (members-at-large). Jews were already barred from membership of the German national society and so, under Jung's new provision, were enabled to join the Society via membership of the individual section. Jung always maintained that his motives for taking on the presidency were to protect Jewish colleagues in this way and to keep depth psychology alive in Germany. Freud's books were burnt and he was 'banned' in 1933.

Jung also became editor of the *Zentralblatt für Psychotherapie*, the Society's scientific journal. This was one of the leading journals of psychotherapy in central Europe. Jung said that this was a *pro forma* appointment and he was geographically distant from the editorial offices. He said he did not know that pro-Nazi statements of principles would be inserted for general distribution outside, as opposed to inside, Germany by Professor Göring (a cousin of the Reichsmarschall) who had been made President of the (dominant) German section.

Jung's own editorials and articles in the *Zentralblatt*, extracts of which appear below, have also been a main reason why he has been accused of pro-Nazi sympathies and anti-semitism. . . .

Having absorbed the contents of the many attacks on Jung, based on the behavior and writing outlined in the previous section entitled 'Background information', my attention was stirred by the nature of the equally numerous defenses of Jung that have been put forward. I found myself reacting to a psychological similarity between the defenses and attacks. Both defenders and attackers of Jung are sitting in judgment on him. Both are looking for a 'final solution' to the

Jung problem. Between the cries of 'Let's clear our man once and for all' and 'Let's finish the bastard off' there is a call for a middle way: Tot up carefully the competing claims of attackers and defenders so as to reach an apparently balanced point of view. It is said that the matter can never be settled decisively. Though it is tempting to join in this Olympian arbitration between attack and defense, that position can be seen as disengaged, morally supercilious, politically evasive, pseudo-mature, and, in any case, as full of a kind of certitude as overt attack or defense! The shadows surrounding Jung are going to linger, for they want us to pay psychological attention to them. . . .

I have recently made a study of one of these co-signed pieces which was published in 1934 (following the matter of the pro-Nazi statement that appeared in the *Zentralblatt* in 1933). Maybe Jung was taken by surprise once again and his name used as co-signatory without permission. We simply cannot know for sure but, as stated above, I do not think that such *lèse-majesté* took place for, if it had, Jung or his associates would have done something about it at the time. The contents of this piece make for instructive reading.

The piece is innocuous-looking–a seventieth-birthday greeting to Dr. Robert Sommer, one of the co-founders in 1926 of the GMSP, by Matthias Göring and Jung. However, Sommer, according to Geoffrey Cocks, was the 'moving spirit' behind attempts to translate the ideas of 'social and racial hygiene' into the mental health field. Sommer founded an organization in 1923 called *Deutscher Verband für Psychische Hygiene* (German Association for Mental Hygiene). In their birthday tribute, Göring and Jung say of this group that it was a 'comparatively small association before the turning-point, today of extraordinary importance'. The 'turning-point' was, of course, the coming to power of the Nazis.

Göring and Jung go on to praise Sommer's book *Familienforschung, Vererbungs- und Rassenlehre* (which can be effectively translated as Family Studies, Hereditology and Raceology–there are no present-day terms for the last two disciplines). In particular, they praise the new chapter of the book, written in 1927 and added to the existing text of 1907. . . . There are several possible reasons why–even if he *did* know what was being published in his journal, sometimes over his name–Jung might still have done nothing in contradiction. First, he might have been in full agreement with these views. But, given the Sommer encomium, that would make him an overt Nazi supporter and rabid 'scientific' anti-semite and he denies both of

these charges. Second, he might have been playing a long-term political game, continuing his strategy of helping Jewish psychotherapists
to go on working. But there is no written or oral evidence that he
held back for this reason and, were it the case, I think that there
would be some evidence. Third, and I believe this is the answer,
Jung's position at the head of the German psychotherapy profession
was desirable from the point of view of the development of analytical
psychology. The issue here is Jung's leadership. After all, Freud had
once written to Jung that psychoanalysis would never find its true
status until it had been accepted in Germany. The conquest of Germany was the goal of the psychoanalytic conquistador. History, and
Hitler, put that goal within Jung's grasp, and I shall look at Jung as
a conquering leader of the field of psychology in the next chapter. . . .

I will argue that the main difficulty with Jung's work in the general
area of national psychology is an unwarranted expansion of his psychology, and hence his authority as a leading psychologist, into complicated fields where psychology on its own is an inadequate explanatory tool, especially concepts like the 'collective unconscious'.

To handle the obvious fact of cultural differences in the forms the
archetypes of the collective unconscious assume, Jung asserted that
there is a 'collective psyche limited to race, tribe, and family over and
above the "universal" collective psyche'. . . .

. . . I certainly do not mean to join in knee-jerk defenses of Jung
here, but we should recognize that, alongside the unfortunate excur-
sions into racial typology, we can also discern the seeds of a surpri-
singly modern and constructive attitude to race and ethnicity. For
example, in 1935 Jung argued against the imposition of 'the spirit' of
one race upon another, referring to a Eurocentric, judgmental approach to other cultures. Here and elsewhere in Jung's writings, there
is also a respect for and interest in the evolution of different cultures. . . .

. . . I hope it becomes clearer why I stress that 'race' is too general
a theme to serve as an overarching backdrop to the drama which has
engulfed Jung. When we look a little more closely at Jung's not-abso-
lutely-collective layer of the collective unconscious, we find that it is
not 'race', not 'tribe', and not 'family' that engage Jung, but *nation*.
Jung makes numerous references to the 'psychology of the nation'
and to the influence of a person's national background, saying that
the 'soil of every country holds [a] mystery . . . there is a relationship
of body to earth'.

When Jung wrote about America and the Americans in 1918, he introduced the idea that the land in or on which an individual lived influenced the psyche and the psychological development of that individual. 'The mystery of the American earth' was so powerful that, according to him, it had even changed the physiognomy of the citizens. The skull and pelvis measurements of second-generation Americans were becoming 'indianized'. Consideration of this absurd idea shows that Jung is not thinking solely along racial lines, for the immigrants from Europe and the indigenous Indians come from *different* races. No–living in America, living on American soil, *being part of the American nation* all exert profound psychological and, according to Jung, physiological effects. Though the effects may be described along roughly racial lines, they have not been caused by race; it is 'the foreign land' that has 'assimilated the conqueror'. . . .

It is my contention that, in C. G. Jung, nationalism found its psychologist and that, in spite of his theoretical concern with the racial unconscious, it is as a psychologist of nationhood that we should also understand Jung's statements about political problems. He was a psychologist who lent his authority to nationalism, thereby legitimizing ideas of innate, psychological differences between nations. Jung's admittedly problematic pan-psychism, the tendency to see all outer events in terms of inner, usually archetypal dynamics, the neglect in his writing of economic, social, political and historical factors, finds its most extreme reductive expression in the phrase 'the psychology of the nation'. . . .

Sensing and recasting Jung as the psychologist of nations does not do away with the problem of his racism. But I suggest that his nationalism is the more important factor in understanding the theoretical overlap which occurs, often at a feeling as much as at a thinking level, between Jung and those Nazis whom he so often asserted did not have his political support and whom, in common with other citizens of Western democracies, he came to fear and hate without reservation.

Jung got into trouble less because of Nazi politics than because of his attempt to write a psychology of nations. We have already seen how complex are the historical, economic, political and cultural forces which go into the development of a nation and its nationalism. Jung's mistake was to expand his role as a psychologist to the point where he could seem to regard the nation as an exclusively psychological fact to be observed solely from a psychological point of view. . . .

It is in this general area that we may understand the response of those who have picked up on the uncomfortable resonances in Jung's writings to something they have already learned to hate in Hitler. Only when we have understood the basis in the collective mind for the association of Hitler's thinking with Jung's can we begin to explicate the enormous divergences between them. Then we can restore the humanity to Jung's quite dissimilar cultural project. . . .

I have criticized Jung for using his leadership and authority as a psychologist for non-psychological purposes. I used the words 'Jung's leadership' deliberately to raise the question of where Jung stood as a leader and in relation to the theory and practice of leadership. The whole subject of leadership, as already stated, forms the second over-arching backdrop to my material.

That Jung had a desire for leadership and behaved like the leader of a movement is still a contentious claim to make within analytical psychology. Many Jungian analysts, recognizing Jung's exceptional gifts, try to put him beyond a power drive, and, therefore, beyond the opportunism to which he is often accused of succumbing in his dealings with the Nazi establishment regulating psychotherapy in Germany in the 1930s. . . .

In the late 1930s Jung was a prime mover in efforts to unite the psychotherapies behind a common program and he drew up a list of propositions concerning the theory and practice of psychotherapy. These 'Fourteen Points', also known as 'Views Held in Common', were Jung's attempt to bring unity to depth psychology. We can see now that the seemingly inherent tendency of depth psychology to fragment into warring groups made this a forlorn hope, practically speaking. But we may well wonder at the idealistic and even arrogant aspects of the use of the political catchphrase dating from the time of the formation of the League of Nations to characterize this effort. Was this an attempt to make Jungian analysis the generic psychotherapy? We know that Jung wanted to be the dominant psychological theorist of the day. He regarded his approach to analysis as *subsuming* those of Adler and Freud (for instance, in his paper 'Problems of modern psychotherapy'). Any Jungian analysis would include the relevant features of an analysis of each of the other schools, although the vital final stage of analysis known as 'transformation' was said to be possible only in Jung's approach. Had the Fourteen Points caught on, Jung would have become the leading theorist of all psychotherapy. . . .

Jung was certainly not completely dominated by his desire for leadership. He did seem able to value other people's points of view and he had a great capacity to tolerate uncertainty and not knowing. He is believable when he says that 'agreement would only spell one-sidedness and desiccation' and that we need many theories before we get 'even a rough picture of the psyche's complexity'. But Jung's élitism is always just below the surface–nature is, after all, 'aristocratic'. The idea of leadership (like that of the nation) forms part of a psychological backdrop to the interplay of Nazis, Jews, Jungians and Freudians that we have been examining. Indeed, in some form this theme pervades *all* these groups. Nazi claims to leadership result in the installation of the Führer with the final solution; there are time-honored Jewish claims to moral primacy as the chosen people; the Freudian Committee, set up in part to ensure that defectors were not taken seriously, illustrates Freudian desires for hegemony; and Jung tried to organize world psychotherapy under his 'neutral' leadership. . . .

At this point, I would like to restate what, for me, is the key question to ask when considering Jung, anti-semitism and the Nazis. Is there anything in Jung's habitual way of thinking that leads to anti-semitism? I think there is–and it is found in the way Jung employs his ideas of the nation and about leadership. These ideas are ideograms with damaging potential and I have tried to show that Jung deployed them in an insufficiently critical manner.

IV: Why was Jung's *Answer to Job* Controversial?

1. Jung's View

Jung to J. B. Priestley, November 8, 1954:*

Jung's friendship with J. B. Priestley promoted a greater awareness of his psychology in Britain. It began in 1946 when Priestley did a BBC radio broadcast on Jung and his work: When Jung saw the transcript he commented that he had never seen a better summary of his main ideas in such a concise form. Later in the same year the English novelist and playwright persuaded Jung to do a talk for the BBC. In 1954 when Jung was about to publish his Answer to Job *in Britain–which his publishers in America had not dared to print–Priestley published two articles (in* The Times Literary Supplement *and* The New Statesman and Nation*) supporting and defending Jung's works. The following selection is an extract from Jung's letter to Priestley, November 8, 1954.*

---

*Jung to Priestley, November 8, 1954, quoted in William Schoenl, *C. G. Jung: His Friendships with Mary Mellon and J. B. Priestley* (Wilmette, Ill.: Chiron Publications, forthcoming). The letter was published in Jung, C. G., *Letters,* ed. Gerhard Adler and Aniela Jaffé, volume 2. Copyright ©1975 by Princeton University Press and Routledge (London). Reprinted by permission of Princeton University Press and Routledge.

You as a writer are in a position to appreciate what it means to an isolated individual like myself to hear one friendly human voice among the stupid and malevolent noises rising from the scribbler-infested jungle. I am indeed most grateful for your warm-hearted support and your generous appreciation. Your succour comes at a time when it is badly needed: soon a little book of mine will be published in England [by Routledge & Kegan Paul] which my publishers in USA [Bollingen Foundation and Pantheon Press] did not dare to print. Its title is: *"Answer to Job."* It deals with the wholly unsatisfactory outcome of the Book of Job and what its further historical consequences for the development of certain religious questions including Christian views were. The book will be highly unwelcome in certain spheres and will be misunderstood and misinterpreted accordingly. The German edition over here has already upset the representatives of three religions [Protestant, Catholic, and Jewish], not because it is irreligious, but because it takes their statements and premises seriously. Needless to say that the best of the so-called free-thinkers are equally shocked. Sir Herbert Read [editor at Routledge & Kegan Paul], who is informed about its contents, wisely said: "You certainly understand how to put the foot into it." But I am really glad that they are willing to print it.

2. Jung on Job

Victor White*

Victor White, a Dominican friar and theologian, became a close friend of Jung. Sometimes criticized by theologians, Jung valued White's theological knowledge and support. A disagreement between the two men arose, however, over White's view of evil as privatio boni *(privation of good), and they fell out with each other. In March 1955 in* Blackfriars *White published sharp criticisms of Jung's* Answer to Job. *Some Jungians have tended to dismiss White's criticisms by referring to his view of evil. Though some may be extreme not all his criticisms can be easily dismissed.*

If ever there were grist for the Jungian mill it was, one might suppose, the Book of Job. It can be read almost as a paradigm of the 'integration process' as Jung himself has repeatedly described it. For here we have a man 'perfect and upright, fearing God and eschewing evil'–as well he might, never having experienced it, and abounding in cosy piety and worldly prosperity. He has, as Satan points out, 'a fence about him, and his house, and his substance'. Anybody can be 'good' in such narrow, sheltered confines as these; but he can hardly be a grown-up man let alone a hero, a prototype of the way of salvation through crucifixion and resurrection. Any psychologist should know he is heading for a crash. Any theologian should know that such easy and complacent virtue cannot continue long in this post-lapsarian world. Job's professed love for God–and God's for

*From Victor White, "Jung on Job," *Blackfriars*, Vol. 36 (March 1955), pp. 52, 54-60. Reprinted by permission.

him–must grow up from this agreeable but infantile and unconscious, autoerotic phase. Job's idol of a merely intelligible and amiable God must be smashed: he must learn the lesson which the New Testament writers were to see it was the function of the Old Testament heroes to teach: that man's righteousness before God is not wrought by moral works without 'faith in the Absurd', the Unseen and the Unknown. So the psychologically and theologically inevitable happens: Job's fences are down; evils rush in. His sufferings are truly frightful, but they are also symptoms; and the loss of his domesticated animals and his children (concerning whose youthful high spirits he had been inordinately anxious), the chidings of the *anima* (his wife), and the psychosomatic eruptions (his boils) add up to a clear clinical picture. He cannot cope. He retires to the dunghill, the libido is introverted, and he is in the grips of intense neurotic depression and conflict. . . .

It has all gone according to schedule: one might almost think that the author had consulted Jung's psychological treatises before writing it. And one might suppose that Dr Jung would be very pleased. But he is not pleased at all; he is very–we might say blindly–angry. So blindly that he gives us a reading of Job no more subtle than that of Bernard Shaw's Black Girl. Jung identifies himself wholly with Job in his sufferings and with his sense of being treated abominably and insanely. His sufferings are just cruel sufferings and in no wise symptoms; only Yahweh is to blame for them. When Elihu appears, it is not at all as a mediator of the unconscious, but just as one heartless idiot more to maintain that Yahweh cannot, in spite of reason and experience, be wrong. . . . Yahweh in any case has nothing to teach Job; he is 'unconscious', 'at odds with himself', contradictory, irritable, irrational, unstable, childishly hungry for love and admiration; in short 'a prehistoric menagerie'. On the contrary, it is Job who 'shows himself superior to his divine partner both intellectually and morally', and it is Job who will, and does, teach God. Yahweh is a slow learner, but after further graded instructions from Ezechiel, Daniel, the Sapiential writers and Enoch, he himself becomes man: not, however, *propter nos homines et propter nostram salutem*, but for his own self-improvement. Unfortunately, however, he incarnates only his 'light side', to the neglect of the 'dark', in the guiltless Christ who 'did no evil'. So the last state is worse than the first: evil is more repressed and unconscious than ever and threatens a terrible revenge. The coming of Christ heralds the reign of Antichrist: the triumph of almighty evil through atomic fission. There are, however, signs that

God is learning better the dark, feminine side of his all too masculine
nature: there is the Woman of the Apocalypse, and there is the papal
definition of the Assumption: hints of a coming, and more satisfac-
tory, rebirth of the God-Man.

The summary of the argument is of course unfair, but no more
astounding than many passages within it. It is not surprising that
some of Jung's friends, jealous for his honour in his old age, and
concerned for the repute and future of his school, have regretted the
publication of this document, or that the German original met with
considerable indignation. Psychiatric journals appear, on the whole,
to have received it with discreet silence. But the *bien pensants*, if not
also the genuinely devout, could hardly restrain their complaints of
impiety and blasphemy. Protestant divines were particularly censor-
ious: they seem not to have read the preface addressed *Lectori Bene-
velo*. But Jung hardly invites their benevolence. Such a *reductio ad
impossibile* of the private interpretation of Scripture, when it really
succeeds in cutting loose from all tradition and every *consensus
fidelium*, must seem a cruel caricature. Nor can it be pleasing to be
told [by Jung] that the Pope's definition of the Assumption is
thoroughly enlightened and up-to-date, while at its critics (the
Anglican Archbishops included) is hurled the supreme insult of being
obscurantist and behind the times–as well as of being deaf to the
Holy Ghost. . . .

. . . Jung has remarked elsewhere that there must be continual
misunderstanding between the theologian and the empirical psychologist over their use of the word 'God'; for 'the theologian will naturally
assume that the metaphysical *Ens Absolutum* is meant', while the empiricist 'just as naturally means a mere statement, at most an archetypal motif which preforms such statements.' It appears, then, that
Jung employs names like 'Yahweh' and nouns like 'God' to function
not as signs but as things (to adopt modern terminology): as second,
not first, *intentiones* (to adopt scholastic terminology). Such usage is
legitimate, though perhaps unusual even among empiricists, but we
must allow Jung to use words in the way he chooses, and (difficult
though it may sometimes be to construe some of his sentences in his
own way) try to understand them accordingly. Thus it emerges from
this preface that in statements about 'God' or 'Yahweh' he is talking
about endopsychic images considered as psychological phenomena
and not as signs for what they merely represent. He is 'quite conscious that . . . none of my reflections touches the essence of the

Unknowable'. He is talking all the time of the interaction between archetypes and ego-consciousness, personifying the former because of their seeming autonomous behaviour. When, for instance, the book says that Yahweh is unconscious, or that aspects of him become conscious, we should understand it to mean that he (or it) is unconscious to the human ego, or that aspects emerge into human consciousness–the only consciousness which the rigid empiricist, who rejects the validity of inference, will recognize. . . .

. . . Although he is not writing of God but God-images, he is not writing directly even of Job's images of God, but rather of his own images of Job's images. This method effectively obscures an objective and dispassionate reading of the Scriptures against their own authentic historical background: it is an interpretation of 'God' at several removes. Its aim is 'not to give a cool and carefully considered exegesis that tries to be fair in every detail, but a purely subjective reaction': to present 'the way in which a modern man with a Christian education and background comes to terms with the divine darkness which is unveiled in the book of Job', Jung will 'not write in a cooly objective manner, but must allow my emotional subjectivity to speak if I want to describe what I feel when I read certain books of the Bible. . . . I shall express my affect fearlessly and ruthlessly.' What he offers us is the highly feeling-toned reaction of 'a layman and a physician who has been privileged to see deeply into the psychic life of many people'. It is an angry book, but it is an anger born of experience and compassion for mankind in its contemporary quandary, and in the disastrous inadequacy of its supposed Christian education to enable it to come to terms with contemporary realities. The preface is headed with the text, 'I am distressed for thee my brother'; and we recall Jung's declaration which, if it cannot win our approval, must yet command our respect:

> 'I do not write for church circles, but for those who stand *extra Ecclesiam*. I associate myself on purpose and deliberately with those who are outside the Church. . . . The Church is my Mother, but the Spirit of my Father draws me away from her into the wide world and its battlefields.'

Even an instructed Christian may expect an explosion when an adult, whose religious development has become fixated at the kindergarten level of bourgeois morality *plus* 'a Friend for little children above the bright blue sky', becomes confronted with the realities of life, of the ways of God both in the Bible and in contemporary events. It is understandable that he feels a close kinship with the disillusioned, tortured Job. Yet it is a fact that the acquaintance of millions of our contemporaries with Christianity has not reached beyond this stage. The violence of the abreaction is understandable, but its infantile quality may still amaze readers who are unfamiliar with abreactions. We might suppose, for instance, that the text, 'Whom the Lord loveth he chastiseth', might call a halt to the tantrums, and even induce the author to reflect that his grievance is hardly adult. But the only reaction is that of the spoiled child: 'It would be quite understandable if the Laodiceans did not *want* too much of this "love".' Other remarks about Christian ideas of love and goodness, otherwise unintelligible or merely abusive (e.g. 'To believe that God is the Summum Bonum is impossible for a reflecting consciousness'), become clear commonsense if they be understood as the reactions of a consciousness which, religiously speaking, has become fixated at the oral phase, for which 'love' means the egotistic 'I want', and 'goodness' only an elementary *bonum delectabile*–perhaps just 'good luck'. . . .

'One would be very ill advised', Jung remarks in quite another connection, 'to identify me with such a childish standpoint.' Nobody who has read his more 'objective' books or who has noted the deep insights in this book–let alone anyone who knows him personally–could make such a mistake about one of the most mature and advanced spirits of our time. Why then, we must ask, does he identify himself with such childish standpoints here? To this there seems no answer except his distress for his brother, his deliberate identification with those *extra Ecclesiam*. An analyst must give his heart to those who suffer and require his aid; and even though he may not lose his head he must run the risk of exposing himself to, and being infected by, their complaints. This book should be neither laughed off nor should it provoke anger or disgust. It does not belong to the large and worthless library written by cranks who wrest the Scriptures to prove some crackpot theory. It has–and this is its most distressing feature–the ingenuity and power, the plausibility and improbability, the clear-sightedness and blindness of the typical paranoid system which rationalizes and conceals an even more unbearable grief and resentment. Its depth and tragedy we can only guess from the fact that it calls upon, not other men, but the hallowed names and symbols of God to carry the projection of the criminal and pathological persecutor. A Christian reader should hear, beneath all the provocation, behind the seeming mockery of all he holds most sacred and most dear, a profoundly moving cry of anguish, a reproachful signal of distress.

But he should also observe that, destructive and childish as much of this book seems to be, its aims are eminently constructive, and that its challenge to ourselves and our contemporaries is imperative and urgent. We must regret that the author seems so often to bark up the wrong tree; but we should see that his attack is essentially directed on Victorian, liberal, diluted, one-sided pictures of God and his Christ which are utterly inadequate to the tasks which our age imposes upon humanity. We can only agree with Jung that these obsolete and insipid idols must be destroyed if a new realization of the God-Man in his wholeness is to be born in human minds and hearts, and humanity itself is to survive. But this precisely is the constant lesson to be drawn from a dispassionate reading of holy Scripture itself, and it is seldom more explicit than in the Book of Job itself. It is also the lesson of the history of the Church, whose task is to carry on and develop 'what Jesus began to do and to teach'–what Jung calls the 'continuing incarnation of God which began with Christ'. We too await another coming of Christ, not in meekness only, but in the full exercise of his power and majesty, and for 'the *hieros gamos*, the marriage of the son with the mother bride.' The pity is that in his violent reaction against an emasculated version of Christianity, he has failed to see that he is, in spite of himself, on the side of the Bible and of authentic orthodox Christianity. Blake wrote of Milton that he was on the devil's side without knowing it; we may say of Jung that he is on Yahweh's side even when he seems to mock at him.

In the very last sentence of the book, when all its *Sturm und Drang* have subsided, Jung leaves us in no doubt that he has known the answer to Job all along:

'Even the enlightened person remains what he is, and is never more than his own limited ego before the One who dwells in him, whose form has no visible boundaries, who encompasses him on all sides, fathomless as the abysms of the earth, and vast as the sky.'

What is this if not–though couched in more modern language–the answer to Job; precisely Yahweh's answer to Job in the Book of Job?

3. *Jung and the Problem of Evil*

H. L. Philp*

H. L. Philp, a British scholar who believed that the psychology of the unconscious was important for theology and pastoral work, corresponded with Jung on the problem of evil. Though appreciative of Jung's psychology he eventually became convinced there were serious weaknesses in Jung's Answer to Job. *He published his criticisms in* Jung and the Problem of Evil *(1958). In the following selection from it he criticizes Jung's lack of knowledge of contemporary Biblical scholarship and takes issue on other points.*

I think that you were perhaps rather unnecessarily obscure in this book, for like many people I have found it, in parts, extremely puzzling. You will remember that this was the common experience of reviewers here and I wrote a letter in your defence to one of our principal literary journals which had bitterly criticized you. I mention this to show that I am not unsympathetic in my approach. I have read *Answer to Job* many times and the general argument I now find easy to follow. . . .

. . .It is important for us to bear in mind that what we are reading about as far as the references to God are concerned are the God-images, the archetype of God. . . .

You realize the difficulties which lie in such a treatment but you make it clear that you are dealing with the archetype of Deity: "It is obvious that this unavoidable dualism will create a certain amount of

*From H. L. Philp, *Jung and the Problem of Evil* (London: Rockliff [Barrie & Jenkins], 1958), pp. 133, 136-137, 165-167. Reprinted with permission.

confusion in the minds of my readers, particularly as in what follows we shall have to do with the archetype of Deity." Most of us in reading your *Answer to Job* find a certain difficulty in spite of this statement because in places you appear to go beyond what you here affirm to be your purpose. You appear to be a lay-theologian, as you assert elsewhere, struggling with the metaphysical problem of evil itself and its relation to the Being of God which is beyond any archetype. You will reply that you are only concerned with what we call our religious experiences and the archetype of Deity. But the distinction does not seem to me to be consistently maintained in your treatment.

One difficulty is caused by the fact that you interpret the Book of Job, as you admit, in an extremely subjective way and not as a Biblical scholar. Yet the book requires for its interpretation all the assistance which the finest Biblical scholarship can give, more especially since the Hebrew text is very imperfect in some parts. Without this knowledge highly personal interpretations can be offered, but it is unlikely that the reader will understand and do justice to the real themes of the book. . . .

The representation which you give of Yahweh in *Answer to Job* is, I believe, a misleading one and far removed from the real picture which we find in the Book of Job itself. You refer to the unconsciousness of God. You say that He is not a 'conscious being' and, in fact, one of your themes is that He wants to become conscious. Dr. Elizabeth Boyden Howes, in her published lecture *Analytical Psychology and the Synoptic Gospels*, referring to your *Answer to Job* interprets your meaning in this way and writes: "God is also to be feared not only because of His threat to our egocentric point of view, but because of His own unpredictability and unconsciousness, because He has within Himself the regressive Satanic side, not wanting to be conscious." You also refer to Yahweh as being amoral. One of the causes of Job's suffering is that God is jealous of him because He fears that man is superior to Him and certainly has a more refined consciousness.

We have to bear in mind that the Book of Job was probably written *circa* 450-350 B.C. We know much about the way Yahweh was thought of by the Hebrews long before this. Amos lived *circa* 760 B.C., Hosea *circa* 740 B.C., Isaiah 740-700 B.C., Jeremiah 626-556 B.C., Ezekiel in the first half of the sixth century B.C., and Deutero-Isaiah soon after the middle of the sixth century B.C. What is the picture then that we find of Yahweh during the period of the prophets? From Amos onwards they restated and stressed the Hebrew conviction that the God of Israel had a unique character. . . .

The God in whom the prophets believed was not capricious as you represent Him to be in your *Answer to Job* but inflexibly righteous. The prophets taught that because we can rely upon this we can always build our life and society on a firm foundation. They also undoubtedly believed that the Yahweh who had this unique character over-ruled the events of history. It was in this faith that they felt that they could stand firm even although the foundations of the earth might appear to be shaken. . . .

I can only conclude, therefore, that the picture which you give of Yahweh in your *Answer to Job* which, as I have stressed, refers to a period later than that of the prophets and so, presumably, to a more advanced stage of revelation, is a misrepresentation of the figure of Yahweh as we find Him both before and during the time of the Book of Job.

4. The Archetypal and Personal Dimensions in *Answer to Job*

Kathleen Newton*

A current perspective on Jung's Answer to Job *is provided by Kathleen Newton. Writing in* The Journal of Analytical Psychology *she examines the personal dimensions as well as the archetypal. Newton cites recent works such as Brian Feldman's article, "Jung's Infancy and Childhood and Its Influence upon the Development of Analytical Psychology" (1992), and Edward F. Edinger's* Transformation of the God-Image: An Elucidation of Jung's *Answer to Job (1992). Her article makes up-to-date and compelling reading on the subject.*

Jung wrote 'Answer to Job' when he was 75 years old after a lifetime's struggle with traditional protestant and religious beliefs, a wide-ranging study of religious symbolism and dialogues with theologians, particularly on the nature of good and evil. He therefore covers many issues, in terms of both metapsychology and theology. Not only that; this is a passionate book written from different angles and from very different places in Jung, and here I am thinking of the clash between his objective understanding response and his highly charged emotional responses. . . .

As I said, the book raises an immensely wide range of complex issues; Jung discusses the problems of the opposites of good and evil

---

*From Kathleen Newton, "The Weapon and the Wound: The Archetypal and Personal Dimensions in 'Answer to Job,' " *The Journal of Analytical Psychology*, Vol. 38 (October 1993), pp. 375, 377-385, 387-389, 391-394. Reprinted by permission of the publisher: Routledge.

and the evolution of the God-image in the *Old* and *New Testament*, including the Book of Revelation. He develops the theme of alchemical symbolism and gives his responses to the Pope's announcement of the dogma of the Assumption of the Virgin Mary. In this paper I will be limiting myself to discussing three questions. The first is to consider Jung's emotional response to the events in the Book of Job and to suggest an alternative way of understanding them. The second is to consider the archetypal and personal significance of the weapon and the wound, and its relation to Jung's personal life; this raises the question of the relationship between intrapsychic and interpersonal dynamics in Jung's psychological development. The third, which overlaps with the second, is to consider the nature of healing: do Jung's emotional responses enable him 'to transform the blindness and the violence on the one hand, and the affect on the other into knowledge'? . . . Here I should say that when I refer to God in this paper I am always referring to man's God-image. . . .

I will now consider an alternative understanding of the events in Job which would be equally valid in terms of Jung's metapsychology. Blake's engravings helped me to 'see with my eyes' some of the issues described in the Bible which Jung ignored. These engravings and Marion Milner's commentaries on them (Milner 1987) have greatly stimulated my thinking about Job, as has Edinger's *Transformation of the God Image* (Edinger 1992).

In the biblical account there are some details to which Jung has turned a blind eye. . . . So here we have a man who is perfect and upright and who continually makes sacrifices on behalf of his children's possible sins. Jung in an objective mood would surely have described this as Job's one-sided conscious attitude and say that he was sustaining his sense of innocence by projecting his shadow onto his children. In fact Jung has a discussion in another part of the book in which he contrasts perfection and completeness and concludes that perfection can only lead to sterility. . . .

. . . one could equally say it is God demonstrating that he is much more than a moral code. In fact, one could say that God's speech illustrates everything which Jung's definition of libido comprises: that is, life energy which flows in predetermined biological, instinctual, mental, moral, and spiritual channels (Jung 1928). Or rather, in so far as morality has dominated a one-sided conscious attitude, he is showing Job the biological, instinctual, and spiritual channels. Looked at in this way we can understand Job's reply, starting 'I had heard of thee by the hearing of the ear', as his recognition that God is much more than a moral good object with whom he can identify, and with this recognition his former self-image, which we could understand as a defensive self, lies in dust and ashes. It is after this recognition that things for Job begin to revive, there is a shift in his orientation and personality. On the one hand, God restores his family and wealth; on the other hand, Job changes from being a powerful man who dispenses charity to a man who can receive gifts from his friends. In addition, the biblical text says: 'And in all the land there were no women found so fair as the daughters of Job, and their father gave them inheritance among their brethren.' So now the feminine principle has become of equal value with the male, an unheard-of thing in those days. With this shift one could think that Job, through his confrontation with the unconscious, has developed in an individuation process (Edinger 1992).

So here are two contrasting ways of relating to the myth. In Jung's emotional response, God is to blame and the challenge is to God to come to terms with his dark side; God is subject and it is God's need which leads to the divine drama culminating in the incarnation in Christ and the crucifixion. In the alternative response, the challenge is to Job's one-sided conscious attitude; the disasters which lead to his descent into despair and the subsequent appearance of God in the whirlwind enable him to achieve a new orientation both intrapsychically and interpersonally. Through his experience he arrives at a deeper knowledge of the instinctual/spiritual dynamics in his God-image which leads to a shift in his attitude to God and also to his values in interpersonal relationships. Here one could say that the achievement of knowledge through suffering has had a healing function which is linked with individuation; it remains open, however, as to what extent Job recognizes that he has a shadow, and it is this recognition which would lead to ego integration. . . .

I will now return to my second question, that is, the archetypal and personal significance of the weapon and the wound and the relevance of the metaphor to Jung's personal life. To take the archetypal motifs first: the motifs which call forth a particularly angry attack on God from Jung are the Garden of Eden myth, Job, and the crucifixion; this last I will return to later, as Jung's responses to the crucifixion are considerably more complex than are those of the former two motifs. . . .

Psychologically, I suggest that the weapon is separation/abandonment in one form or another, whether in physical terms or emotional unavailability, and the wound is the narcissistic wound to the protagonist's sense of identity and the pain and outrage which this engenders. The pain is symbolized in the myths I have referred to; in the Garden of Eden myth, pain about the conflict and disillusion which arises on the awakening of consciousness, and in Job, pain about the loss of a good object in whom one's sense of identity resides . . . .

In order to follow up the personal dimension in Jung's emotional responses to Job I have selected incidents from *Memories, Dreams, Reflections* which link the child Jung's extremely vulnerable sense of identity with his narcissistic wounds. They illustrate both the healing and the defensive structures which he established to survive conflict and have a bearing on my second and third questions. From his memories it is very clear that we can relate the archetypal motif of abandonment and 'the weapon and the wound' to his personal experience. Feldman, in his discussion of Jung's childhood, highlights Jung's need 'to turn inward to find his own sources of healing as the early interpersonal environment could not provide him with a sense of security which would engender trust'. . . .

The difficulties in his parent's marriage were a central issue in Jung's childhood. In his view his mother's depression and hospitalization when he was 3 years old were due to the tension in the marriage relationship. In addition one can conjecture that his mother's depression had led to a difficult early relationship with the infant Jung and his reaction to her hospitalization was extreme.

> From then on I always felt mistrustful when the word love was spoken. The feeling I associated with women was, for a long time, that of innate unreliability. Father, on the other hand, was reliable but powerless.

So one can understand this as a savage wound to Jung's capacity to love and trust in a personal relationship, and as he grew older his split perception of his mother was a further source of alienation. By day she was an extroverted warm person, albeit with a No. 1 and No. 2 personality with whom Jung could not have an open exchange; at night she was uncanny. Given the tensions and anxieties between his parents, there was no way in which ambivalent feelings of love and aggression could be safely expressed, and the child Jung retreated into his very rich inner world. . . .

. . . An incident of a rather different kind was Jung's intense conflict about his fantasy of God's turd breaking 'the walls of the cathedral asunder'. As Feldman says, we can understand this as Jung's narcissistic rage against both his parents (Feldman 1992). Jung, however, had no personal associations of this sort, on the contrary for him it raised the whole question of a good God and sin; 'a God who could do something terrible'. Equally he had a polarized response to this experience. On the one hand, 'I felt an enormous, an indescribable relief. Instead of the expected damnation, grace had come upon me, and with it unutterable bliss such as I had never known . . . It was as though I had experienced an illumination . . . That was what my father had not understood.' On the other hand, 'I had experienced a dark and terrible secret. It overshadowed my whole life, and I became deeply pensive.' The experience also had the effect of polarizing Jung's self-image. 'I am a devil or a swine . . . I am infinitely depraved.' 'As a result, I had the feeling that I was either outlawed or elect, accursed or blessed.' In this experience Jung's anal aggression was projected into his God-image and so it remained a split-off omnipotent fantasy. As long as Jung's God-image is subject and it is God's turd that attacks the temple there is no potential for ego integration and the erotic aggressive opposites remain in the form of archetypal absolutes. . . .

As we know, in Jung's adolescence, the deprivation in interpersonal exchange was reinforced. It was after his confirmation that Jung realized that he 'couldn't believe a word that his father said'. His attempts at discussion about religion were always evaded. To make matters more difficult Jung became more and more aware of his father's vulnerability and pain about his loss of faith. Given these difficulties Jung's pattern of turning to his inner world was reinforced; there was no way he could work through disagreements in a personal relationship. One could say that from the time of the phallus dream Jung's relationship with his father was bypassed. It was his identification with an old wise man figure, his experience of his No. 2 personality, and his relationship to God which were central. Later of course there was a repeat in the intense relationship and final disagreements with Freud when, as Winnicott put it, there could not be an imaginative clash, there had to be a complete break (Winnicott 1964). It was alongside, and after the relationship with Freud finished, that the dreams and fantasies described in the chapter on the confrontation with the unconscious in *Memories, Dreams, Reflections* were so powerful that Jung knew there was a danger of psychosis. Here again Jung did not make the link that these fantasies might have had with his personal conflicts over his break with Freud. Satinover makes a very convincing case for the relationship between the two (Satinover 1985). It seems worth noting that, at this stage of his life, Jung did value his family relationships and his relationships with his patients as having a supportive function, a proof that he was 'normal'.

According to his own account therefore Jung could only survive the early and later narcissistic wounds of abandonment, which threatened him with disintegration, by turning to intrapsychic activities with his powerful fantasies and dreams. He says that he held on to his childhood memories because they provided him with 'a secret truth which enabled him to preserve a sense of the privacy and integrity of his developing self'. In that sense they served a vital healing function. In continuing on this path, and in his search to find meaning, he was able to acquire an immense amount of knowledge about archetypal motifs and unconscious processes, which did lead to important creative discoveries about the collective unconscious and the archetypal dynamics in the psyche. On the other hand, in so far as these discoveries also served as a defence against emotional conflicts in interpersonal relationships, these conflicts did not get addressed (Jacoby 1981). This meant a loss in terms of a potential for healing through ego integration, and Jung left us with a polarization both between the personal and collective unconscious and the causal infantile reductive/archetypal teleological synthetic approaches which post-Jungians have continued to work on and integrate. . . .

. . . 'All opposites are of God, therefore man must bend to this burden; and in so doing he finds God in his "oppositeness" has . . . incarnated himself in him . . . the conscious recognition of the opposites, painful though it may be at the moment, does bring with it a definite feeling of deliverance . . . from the distressing state of dull and helpless unconsciousness' (Jung 1952, para. 659). Jung does not apply this statement to Job's 'moral superiority' but, in making it, it would seem that giving vent to his rage with God has served a purpose; for in this statement, there is a breakthrough. Man is no longer an innocent victim, and suffering is linked with his recognition of his own shadow. Man, and here one could say Jung, has now become subject both in relation to God in his opposites and the opposites in his own nature and has thus loosened the moral sado-masochistic tie between the weapon and the wound and the global opposites of innocence and guilt. In fact, with this understanding it would seem that Jung had arrived at an approximation to Job's position at the end of the Job story. The two have got there by different routes. Job's experience of abandonment by an all-good moral God, his descent into despair and confrontation with God the creator of the universe, led him to lose and/or relinquish his defensive narcissistic self-image and find a new orientation in both intrapsychic and interpersonal terms. Jung, through giving vent to his anger with God on Job's behalf, has been able to express feelings which he could not live interpersonally in his relationship with his parents in response to his own narcissistic wound. Through experiencing the violence in his response he achieved an ego position which enabled him to relinquish his (and if he chose to link it, Job's) moral superiority to his God-image and accept the opposites in terms of his own feelings. Rather than God's turd destroying the cathedral, Jung has experienced his turd attacking God. . . .

. . . However, if one thinks of the individuation process as one in which we spiral round the same conflicts, hopefully arriving at a deeper quality of emotional integration, one could say that Jung, in his angry attack on God, had travelled along this path. In his childhood experience he felt an object, a victim 'accursed or blessed', hence his identification with Job. In 'Answer to Job' he could attack God and in doing this he experienced himself as subject. In so far as the attack shifted from that of moral outrage to recognition of the opposites in his own nature, he achieved an ego position with a potential for integration. Translated into developmental terms we could think of the depressive position, with God as an intrapsychic substitute for the interpersonal relationship primarily with his mother and later with his father. Here the balance between intrapsychic and interpersonal dynamics would seem crucial. Omnipotent archetypally derived fantasies, such as Jung had in his childhood, have both collective and personal implications, and following up the meaning in either context can serve a healing function. However, if the absolute archetypal opposites of good and evil, innocence and guilt, are to be translated into personal affects, one needs to experience love, hate, and guilt in an interpersonal context, in which there is an ongoing potential for concern and reparation. A process which we could associate with integrating the shadow.

I suggest that we can understand Jung's emotional responses in 'Answer to Job' as belonging to overlapping levels of experience. First, he is giving expression to his split-off, pent-up narcissistic pain and outrage with his mother's betrayal, and later his father's unavailability in terms of personal exchange. In that sense he is giving expression to the affective roots of personal/archetypal experience in infancy and childhood. Second, I think he is expressing anger at the collapse of his own defensive structures at those times when he identified with an idealized self-image, in moments of feeling whole, and when identified with the 'Other' No. 2 personality as exclusively good, a 'haven of peace and solitude'. Here one has to value the creativity in these experiences while also recognizing when they are being idealized and used defensively (Redfearn 1985). Given Jung's childhood memories this was an ongoing conflict for him. On another level Jung was continuing his battle with orthodox Christian doctrine; the fact that the emotional roots in this battle stemmed from early childhood experience may, but does not necessarily, undermine the outcome and may enrich the validity of the position which he arrives at and the creativity in the ongoing battle. Lastly, Jung's response would seem to belong to the conflict of opposites with which reality confronts us. . . .

I am well aware that in following up the three main questions which 'Answer to Job' raised for me, I have not done justice to Jung as a whole, or the book as a whole. However, I think that the themes on which I have focused do throw light on my second and third questions. . . . Jung, in both following up the transformation of the God-image in the divine drama, and giving free rein to his feelings, has enabled us to meet him in the round both in terms of his creativity and his shadow. In doing this he has left us all in a better position to find our personal equation in the archetypal and personal dimensions in his answers to Job and to the conflict of opposites with which we are all confronted.

Notes

I.1. *The Freud/Jung Letters: The Correspondence between Sigmund Freud and C. G. Jung*, ed. William McGuire, tr. Ralph Manheim and R. F. C. Hull, Bollingen Series XCIV (Princeton: Princeton University Press, 1974), pp. 525–527.

I.2. *The Complete Correspondence of Sigmund Freud and Ernest Jones, 1908–1939*, ed. R. Andrew Paskauskas (Cambridge, Mass. and London, Eng.: Belknap Press of Harvard University Press, 1993), pp. 180, 182.

I.3. C. G. Jung, *Analytical Psychology: Notes of the Seminar Given in 1925*, ed. William McGuire, Bollingen Series XCIX (Princeton: Princeton University Press, and London: Routledge, 1989), pp. 19–25.

I.4. Brian Feldman, "Jung's Infancy and Childhood and Its Influence upon the Development of Analytical Psychology," *The Journal of Analytical Psychology*, Vol. 37 (July 1992), pp. 255, 257–258, 261–262, 265–267, 271–273.

II.1. Jung, *Psychology and Religion*, originally published in English: The Terry Lectures of 1937 at Yale University (1938), revised in accordance with the Swiss edition (1940) in *The Collected Works of C. G. Jung*, Volume 11: *Psychology and Religion* (Princeton: Princeton University Press, 2nd ed., 1969), paragraphs 2–5, 11, 14–16, 26, 36–37, 41.

II.2. Walter Kaufmann, *Discovering the Mind*, Vol. 3: *Freud versus Adler and Jung* (New York: McGraw-Hill, 1980), pp. 397–398, 426–427, 429.

II.3. J. J. Clarke, *In Search of Jung* (London and New York: Routledge, 1992), pp. xiii–xiv, 4, 9–11, 22, 35, 37–38, 74, 116, 128–129.

II.4. Barbara Stephens, review of *The Jung Cult* by Richard Noll, *Psychological Perspectives*, Issue 31 (Spring–Summer 1995), pp. 142–145.

III.1. Jung, "Editorial (1933)," published in the *Zentralblatt für Psychotherapie und ihre Grenzgebiete* (Leipzig), VI:3 (December 1933), pp. 139–140, trans. and published in Jung, *Civilization in Transition*, Vol. 10 of *The Collected Works of C. G. Jung*, 2nd ed. (Princeton: Princeton University Press, 1970, rpt. 1975), paragraphs 1014–1015.

III.2. Geoffrey Cocks, *Psychotherapy in the Third Reich*, 2nd edition (New Brunswick, NJ: Transaction Publishers, forthcoming).

III.3. Jung to Mary Mellon, September 24, 1945, quoted in William Schoenl, *C. G. Jung: His Friendships with Mary Mellon and J. B. Priestley* (Wilmette, Ill.: Chiron Publications, forthcoming).

III.4. Aryeh Maidenbaum, "Preface," in *Lingering Shadows: Jungians, Freudians, and Anti-Semitism*, ed. Maidenbaum and Stephen A. Martin (Boston & London: Shambhala, 1991), pp. ix–xii.

III.5. Andrew Samuels, *The Political Psyche* (London and New York: Routledge, 1993), pp. 287–292, 294, 298–300, 307–311, 313–315, 320-325.

IV.1. Jung to Priestley, November 8, 1954, quoted in William Schoenl, *C. G. Jung: His Friendships with Mary Mellon and J. B. Priestley* (Wilmette, Ill.: Chiron Publications, forthcoming). This letter was published in Jung, *Letters*, ed. Gerhard Adler and Aniela Jaffé, volume 2 (Princeton: Princeton University Press, and London: Routledge, 1975).

IV.2. Victor White, "Jung on Job," *Blackfriars*, Vol. 36 (March 1955), pp. 52, 54–60.

IV.3. H. L. Philp, *Jung and the Problem of Evil* (London: Rockliff [Barrie & Jenkins], 1958), pp. 133, 136–137, 165–167.

IV.4. Kathleen Newton, "The Weapon and the Wound: The Archetypal and Personal Dimensions in 'Answer to Job,'" *The Journal of Analytical Psychology*, Vol. 38 (October 1993), pp. 375, 377–385, 387–389, 391–394.

Suggestions for Additional Reading

This bibliography must be selective. It represents only a portion of the literature on Jung's life and work. I have suggested works that I and participants in my seminars found useful in addition to the works excerpted above. Readers, of course, might have other selections.

A good starting point on the issue of Jung's break with Freud is his *Memories, Dreams, Reflections* (New York, 1962), particularly Ch. 5, "Sigmund Freud." In addition to *The Freud/Jung Letters* other primary sources include: *C. G. Jung: Letters*, ed. Gerhard Adler, Vol. 1: 1906-1950 (Princeton, 1973), and on the Freudian side–besides *The Complete Correspondence of Sigmund Freud and Ernest Jones, 1908-1939–The Correspondence of Sigmund Freud and Sándor Ferenczi*, ed. Eva Brabant *et al.*, Volume 1: 1908-1914 (Cambridge, Mass., 1993), *A Psycho-Analytic Dialogue: The Letters of Sigmund Freud and Karl Abraham, 1907-1926*, ed. Hilda C. Abraham and Ernst L. Freud (London, 1965), and *Sigmund Freud: Letters*, ed. Ernst L. Freud (New York, 1960). Jones, Ferenczi, and Abraham, together with Otto Rank and Hanns Sachs, were members of the "Committee," a small guard of "trustworthy analysts" around Freud.

John Kerr's *A Most Dangerous Method: The Story of Jung, Freud, and Sabina Spielrein* (New York, 1993) is a fascinating history of her role in the Jung-Freud relations and of the founding period of the psychoanalytic movement. Gerhard Wehr, Jung's recent biographer, *Jung: A Biography* (Boston, 1987), discusses the break; Peter Gay, Freud's recent biographer, *Freud: A Life for Our Time* (New York, 1988), presents a very pro-Freudian account. Among older works readers might sample: Neil Wollman, "Contrasts between Jung and Freud: The Intertwining of Life and Theory," *The Journal of Analytical Psychology*, 29 (April 1984), 171-186; Vincent Brome, *Freud and His Disciples* (London, 1984); George B. Hogenson, *Jung's Struggle with Freud* (Notre Dame, 1983); Robert S. Steele, *Freud and*

Jung: Conflicts of Interpretation (London, 1982); and Vincent Brome, *Jung* (London, 1978).

J. J. Clarke's *In Search of Jung*, from which excerpts have been printed above, might well serve as an introduction to further reading on whether Jung was empirical or mystical. Richard Noll, *The Jung Cult: Origins of a Charismatic Movement* (Princeton, 1994), is a recent challenge to the view that Jung was empirical–and to the theory of the collective unconscious. Wolfgang Pauli and C. G. Jung, *Ein Briefwechsel*, ed. C. A. Meier (Heidelberg, 1992) is the recently published correspondence between Jung and the Nobel prize-winning physicist Pauli. Critiques of Jung's work may be found in: A. Stevens, *Jung* (Oxford, 1994) and *On Jung* (London, 1990); D. McGowan, *What Is Wrong with Jung* (Buffalo, 1994); G. Masson, *Against Therapy* (London, 1989); W. A. Shelburne, *Mythos and Logos in the Thought of Carl Jung: The Theory of the Collective Unconscious in Scientific Perspective* (Albany, 1988); L. S. Hearnshaw, *The Shaping of Modern Psychology* (London, 1987); A. Samuels, *Jung and the Post-Jungians* (London, 1985); M. Stein, *Jung's Treatment of Christianity: The Psychotherapy of a Religious Tradition* (Wilmette, Ill., 1985); R. K. Papadopoulos and G. S. Saayman, eds., *Jung in Modern Perspective* (Hounslow, 1984); C. Wilson, *C. G. Jung: Lord of the Underworld* (Wellingborough, 1984); A. Stevens, *Archetypes: A Natural History of the Self* (London, 1982); S. S. Hughes, *Consciousness and Society: The Reorientation of European Social Thought, 1890-1930* (Brighton, 1979); P. Rieff, *The Triumph of the Therapeutic: Uses of Faith after Freud* (Harmondsworth, 1973); A. Storr, *Jung* (London, 1973); J. Hillman, *The Myth of Analysis: Three Essays in Archetypal Psychology* (New York, 1972); C. Rycroft, *A Critical Dictionary of Psychoanalysis* (Harmondsworth, 1972); E. Jones, *The Life and Work of Sigmund Freud*, one volume edited and abridged by L. Trilling (Harmondsworth, 1964); and R. S. Peters, ed., *Brett's History of Psychology* (London, 1962).

On the issue whether Jung was, for a time, "a Nazi sympathizer" or not, after his "Editorial 1933" readers might wish to see his "Rejoinder to Dr. Bally" (1934), "The State of Psychotherapy Today" (1934), and "Circular Letter (1934)" in Vol. 10 of *The Collected Works of C. G. Jung* (New York, 1964; rpt. Princeton, 1970). Besides Jung's letter to Mary Mellon, September 24, 1945, other materials that have recently come to light include a birthday greeting praising Dr. Robert Sommer co-signed by Dr. Matthias Göring and Jung in 1934; Jung's relationship with Wilhelm Hauer, professor of Indology and founder of the German Faith Movement in 1933; and Jung's birthday greetings to Matthias Göring in 1939. See Andrew Samuels, "New Materials concerning Jung, Anti-Semitism, and the Nazis," *The Journal of Analytical Psychology*, 38 (October 1993), 463-470, and, in the same issue, Matthias von der Tann *et al.*, "Jung's Birthday Greetings to Professor Göring," pp. 471-473. Andrew Samuels' *The Political Psyche*, Aryeh Maidenbaum and Stephen A. Martin's *Lingering Shadows: Jungians, Freudians, and Anti-Semitism*, and Geoffrey Cocks' *Psychotherapy in the Third Reich* are indispensable reading. M. von der Tann and A. Erlenmeyer, *C. G. Jung und der Nationalsozialismus*, 2nd ed. (Berlin, 1993) may be obtained from the German Society of Analytical Psychology. Martine Gallard, "Jung's Attitude during the Second World War in the Light of the Historical and Professional Context," *The Journal of Analytical Psychology*, 39 (April 1994), 203-232, is mistitled: It is mainly about Jung's attitude *before* World War II. It goes over many of the facts already discussed by Andrew Samuels, "National Psychology, National Socialism, and Analytical Psychology: Reflections on Jung and Anti-Semitism," in the same journal, 37 (April 1992), 127-147, and 37 (January 1992), 3-28. Among the older articles readers might examine: Jay Sherry, "Jung, the Jews, and Hitler," *Spring: An Annual of Archetypal Psychology and Jungian Thought* (1986), pp. 163-175; James Kirsch, "Jung's Transference on Freud: Its Jewish Element," *American Imago: A Psychoanalytic Journal for Culture, Science, and the Arts*, 41 (Spring 1984), 63-84; Geoffrey Cocks, "C. G. Jung and German Psychotherapy, 1933-1940," *Spring* (1979), pp. 221-227; and Clarence J. Karier, "The Ethics of a Therapeutic Man: C. G. Jung," *The Psychoanalytic Review*, 63 (Spring 1976), 115-146.

A good starting point on why Jung's *Answer to Job* was controversial is, of course, the work itself: *Antwort auf Hiob*, German edition (Zurich, 1952); *Answer to Job*, English edition (London, 1954). The work was republished in Vol. 11 of *The Collected Works of C. G . Jung* (New York, 1958, rpt. 1969). *C. G. Jung: Letters*, ed. Gerhard Adler, Vol. 2: 1951-1961 (Princeton, 1975), may be combed for Jung's feelings about responses to his *Answer to Job*.

In addition to Kathleen Newton's recent article in *The Journal of Analytical Psychology*, Eli Weisstub's "Questions to Jung on 'Answer to Job,'" appeared in the same issue, 38 (October 1993), 397-418. The well-known Jungian Edward F. Edinger earlier published *Trans-*

formation of the God-Image: An Elucidation of Jung's Answer to Job (Toronto, 1992). Ann Conrad Lammers, *In God's Shadow: The Collaboration of Victor White and C. G. Jung* (Mahway, N. J., 1994), is an account of Jung's relationship with White. Among older works readers might examine: James Forsyth, *Freud, Jung and Christianity* (Ottawa, 1989); Murray Stein and Robert L. Moore, eds., *Jung's Challenge to Contemporary Religion* (Wilmette, Ill., 1987); and Luther H. Martin and James Goss, eds., *Essays on Jung and the Study of Religion* (Lanham, Md., 1985). Victor White, who criticized *Answer to Job*, also wrote *Soul and Psyche: An Enquiry into the Relationship of Psychotherapy and Religion* (London, 1960): Its Appendix 5, "Jung on Job," is a revised version of his article that appeared in *Blackfriars*, March 1955. Martin Buber, the eminent Jewish existentialist, *Eclipse of God* (1952) and C. G. Jung, "Religion and Psychology [1952]: A Reply to Martin Buber," reprinted in Vol. 18 of *The Collected Works of C. G. Jung* (Princeton, 1975), though not directly on *Answer to Job*, remain well worth reading.